GARDENING WITHOUT WORK

for the aging, the busy and the indolent

by

Ruth Stout

Line drawings by Nan Stone

CORNERSTONE LIBRARY • NEW YORK

Reprinted 1974

This new Cornerstone Library edition is published by arrangement
with Devin-Adair Company, and is a complete unabridged reprint of
the original hardcover edition.

Some of the material in this book has appeared in the following magazines: *Organic Gardening and Farming*, Emmaus, Pa.;
Popular Gardening, New York City; and *Natural Food and Farming*, Atlanta, Texas. Acknowledgment and thanks are hereby
extended.

for Dick
(Professor Richard V. Clemence to you)
with gratitude and affection

CORNERSTONE LIBRARY PUBLICATIONS
Are Distributed By
Simon & Schuster, Inc.
630 Fifth Avenue
New York, N.Y. 10020
Manufactured in the United States of America
under the supervision of
Rolls Offset Printing Co., Inc., N.Y.

Contents

. . . . . *Also crows ignore corn which is either planted this way or which has hay thrown on top of it immediately after it's planted: (See page 34)*

1

God invented mulching

Some years ago I wrote a short article, which appeared in a national magazine, telling about how I had been successfully growing flowers and vegetables for quite a long time with almost no labor but planting and picking. I wasn't swamped with fan mail, but I did get enough excited letters from gardeners all over the United States to make me feel that I had an obligation to the millions of others who hadn't read the article. Also to those who may have read it but needed a worthwhile push to get them started.

I have always liked that prayer which asks for the courage to change those things which we can, for the serenity to accept the ones we cannot change, and for the wisdom to know the difference between the two. Well, here was a situation I could at least try to change; I could write a book about this easy way of gardening.

I finished the first chapter and sent it to my sister to read and comment on. She returned it, saying in effect: You told the whole story in a 1500-word article; how do you expect to fill a book?

I had foreseen that difficulty, had been wondering how on earth I could. But the publisher who was interested in the project suggested that I tell about the hard work, and the struggle, and the various crop failures I had endured during the fourteen years of growing things the old-fashioned way, showing the contrast between it and the new method. Following this advice I had no trouble filling a book which we called *How to Have a Green Thumb Without an Aching Back* which was published by *Exposition Press*. And being an incurable optimist, I had visions of cluttering up the lives of all gardeners with leisure. One day my publisher said to me:

"Say, stop dreaming. I may sell a few million copies for

you, but you aren't going to revolutionize gardening."

Well, I wonder. That was several years ago and he is still plugging away on the first million, but garden magazines and farm papers are spreading the glad tidings, and I still, after five years, get a few letters every day from happy converts. More than one librarian has told me that people who borrow my book don't want to part with it; they return it, then, in plain language, they steal it from the shelf. A man who went into the spoiled hay business when my method (which is a year-round mulch) got popular, told me that when he began to run short and had to turn down orders, someone sneaked in and helped himself. And a dentist in Pennsylvania and a doctor in Oregon have both written me that they keep a copy of my garden book in their waiting rooms. Or at least try to; the dentist has had twenty-three copies stolen, the doctor, sixteen.

I am not exactly boasting that my idea turns people into thieves, but I can scarcely help feeling flattered. It's a fair-sized job to write a book that people can be bothered just to read; when they begin to steal copies of one you've written, you are really getting some place.

But since I had a problem about filling one small volume, why do I write another? There are two answers to that; one is that a few points I made could do with some clarifying, but the important reason is that I have learned a great deal from the people who have written me and from those who have come to see my method in action. I feel that these experiences and this information should be passed along, although much of it will necessarily be secondhand knowledge; in each case I shall make that distinction. I mustn't fall into the habit which I so often deplore—that of laying down laws and making positive statements with no personal first-hand knowledge back of them. I will modify that: I feel that laying down strict laws is bad gardening practice under almost any circumstances.

Over fifteen hundred gardeners have come for a first-hand look at my method, more than four thousand others have written to me, and I have no idea how many thousands of people I have given so-called lectures to; my talk lasts for about fifteen minutes, then I ask for questions and comments. All this means that by now I have a fairly accurate idea not only of the points in my book which need some clarification or elaboration, but also of some other points which gardeners want to know and which I didn't touch on.

When, overnight, I became an "authority," my outspoken husband, Fred Rossiter, said to me: "You are going to be asked ten thousand questions which you can't answer." True enough, but I do have what it takes to say "I don't know," instead of floundering around in an effort to find a reasonable facsimile of an answer.

Fred has a scientific approach to a subject; at first he couldn't believe that my ignoring of the experts wouldn't get me into trouble, and when gardeners drove in he would go to the patch with us to lend a helping tongue. Since I write under my maiden name some of the visitors called Fred "Mr. Stout"; one of our friends asked him if he minded and he replied: "Oh no, I'm used to it, but the first guy who calls me Mr. Mulch is going out on his ear."

And now let's get down to business. The labor-saving part of my system is that I never plow, spade, sow a cover crop, harrow, hoe, cultivate, weed, water or irrigate, or spray. I use just one fertilizer (cotton seed or soy bean meal), and I don't go through that tortuous business of building a compost pile. Just yesterday, under the "Ques-

. . . *After I read this I lay there on the couch and suffered because the victim's address wasn't given: there was no way I could reach him.*

tions and Answers" in a big reputable farm paper, someone asked how to make a compost pile and the editor explained the arduous performance. After I read this I lay there on the couch and suffered because the victim's address wasn't given; there was no way I could reach him.

My way is simply to keep a thick mulch of any vegetable matter that rots on both my vegetable and flower garden all year round. As it decays and enriches the soil, I add more.

And I beg everyone to start with a mulch eight inches deep; otherwise, weeds may come through, and it would be a pity to be discouraged at the very start. But when I am asked how many bales (or tons) of hay are necessary to cover any given area I can't answer from my own experience, for I gardened in this way for years before I had any idea of writing about it, and therefore didn't keep track of such details. However, I now have some information on this from Dick Clemence, my A-number-one adviser, whom I will tell you about in a later chapter. He says: "Hay is such a variable commodity that any useful advice on quantities must be understood to refer to orders of magnitude only. I should think of twenty-five fifty-pound bales as about the minimum for an area 50' x 50', or about a half-ton of loose hay. That should give a fair starting cover, but an equal quantity in reserve would be desirable. Starting in the summer on sod, the whole business should go on at once—fifty bales, or a ton of loose hay. The experienced gardener can effect economies, and manage with less, but beginners do well to have plenty of hay available."

That is a better answer than the one I have been giving people, which is: you need at least twice as much as you would think.

Once the editor of a garden magazine asked me to send him an article on some aspect of my method, and when I suggested one on how I plan my garden in advance on paper, he answered: "Fine, but I didn't think you did any planning; I had an idea that you just went out, whenever you were in the mood, and scattered seeds around over the hay."

He was joking, but it astonishes me how many people who have read my book through get almost that same impression. I was beginning to get disgusted with myself for

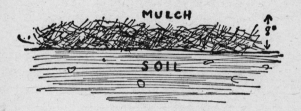

HOW MUCH MULCH ?

And I beg everyone to start with a mulch eight inches deep; . . . . .

apparently not making it clear how one plants when using my system, and I looked through the chapter called *Throw Away Your Spade and Hoe,* to find out just how careless I had been. But there it is on page 69: ". . . I had to rake away the mulch in order to plant . . . make a tiny furrow and drop the seeds."

Whenever I am asked this question (and I still often am) I reply: "You plant exactly as you always have—*in the earth.* You pull back the mulch and put the seeds in the ground and cover them just as you would if you had never heard of mulching." When I am replying in writing to someone who has asked this question by mail, I underscore heavily; when I am talking to a garden group I try not to shout it but I probably do. When the questioner is there in my garden, I get down on my knees and give a demonstration.

Then the next thing I have to straighten various people out on is whether or not you put mulch on top of the planted seeds. In the beginning I was a little amazed that anyone could ask such a foolish question, but someone who

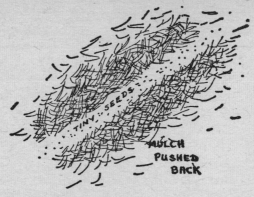

. . . . You pull back the mulch and put the seeds in the ground and cover them just as you would if you had never heard of mulching.

was following my system did some experimenting on his own, and discovered that one could put hay on top of the larger seeds immediately after they were planted. This has some definite advantages, which I will tell about later.

I carefully do not put any mulch on top of tiny seeds, such as lettuce and parsley, but I do pull it right back up to the row after I plant. Recently I had some information about planting small seeds, but I have had a chance to try that only once, so I will put it in chapter VIII, where I tell about the experiences of other gardeners.

Over and over I am asked why it isn't bad to mulch with hay which is full of weed seeds. The answer to this is that if the mulch is thick enough, the weeds can't come through. Invariably someone in an audience will then ask why the vegetable seeds come through, while weed seeds don't, and I explain once more (with angelic patience) that the mulch is on top of the weed seeds but not on top of the small vegetable seeds.

One man, in a group I was talking to, was determined not to let me get away with claiming that it was all right to throw a lot of hay full of grass seeds on one's garden, and the rest of the audience was with him. I was getting nowhere and was bordering on desperation, when, finally, I asked him:

"If you were going to make a lawn, would you plant the grass seed and then cover it with several inches of hay?" Put that way he at last realized that a lot of hay on top of tiny seeds would keep them from germinating.

However, it's true that you can lay chunks of baled hay between the rows of vegetables in your garden and, in a wet season, have a hearty growth of grass right on top of the hay. All you need do is turn the chunk of hay over. Now this isn't much of a job but some ardent disciples of my system are capable of getting indignant with me (in a nice way, of course) because they are put to that bother. I have relieved them of all plowing, hoeing, cultivating, weeding, watering, spraying, making compost piles; how is it that I haven't thought of some way to avoid this turning over of those chunks of hay?

One question I am often asked is: how can you safely plant little seeds between eight-inch walls of mulch? One can't, of course, but almost before one gets through spreading it, the mulch begins to settle and soon becomes a two or three inch compact mass rather than an eight-inch fluffy one. It will no doubt be walked on, and rain may come; in any case, it will settle. As a matter of fact you won't need eight inches to start if you use solid chunks of baled hay.

Many people want to know why I don't use manure and what I have against it. I have nothing at all against it; in fact, I have a somewhat exaggerated respect for it. But I no longer need it; the ever-rotting mulch takes its place. I sort of complained, in my first book, that no one ever wrote an ode to manure, and through the years since then at least a half-dozen people have sent me poems which they composed about manure piles.

I have been asked over and over if such things as sawdust and oak leaves should be avoided, the idea being that they make the soil too acid. I use sawdust, primarily around raspberries, with excellent results. We have no oak trees, therefore I can't answer that question from experience, but

I certainly wouldn't hesitate to use them; then, if it turned out that they were making the soil acid, I would add some wood ashes or lime. I've had reports from a great many gardeners who have used both sawdust and oak leaves over their entire garden and have found them satisfactory.

I devoted a whole chapter to strawberries in that first book and I might as well have saved myself the trouble. With extra pains I described how I grow them in a permanent bed, then, to make sure that what I said was clear, I asked several people to read my explanation, trying it out on some who grew berries and on others who never had. When I got the chapter fixed up so that it satisfied everyone, I was sure it was foolproof.

But I can't tell you how many people have written and asked me for further details, begging for diagrams. More than that, even many visitors who were standing there in my garden, looking at the bed, found the idea difficult to grasp. And so I thought up a simpler way to have a permanent strawberry bed, easier to explain, and easier, too, for me to practice, and here it is. If you don't understand it, please don't write to me about it; think up one of your own, which I'm sure you can.

If you are making a new bed set the plants three feet apart in a row and space the runners one foot apart, cutting off all superfluous ones. Then, after you have picked your first crop, thin the bed by pulling out all the least-promising-looking plants, and some others, too, if too many look promising. Let the new runners fill the vacant spots, and cut off all other runners. Isn't that easy?

To some of you this will happen: you will get involved with other work and/or pleasures and the runners will get ahead of you; in the fall you will feel conscience-stricken and perhaps defeated at the look of your berry patch and may go back to the old way of putting in a new bed each year. Or you may even give up growing strawberries.

Before you do either, I suggest that you try this: abandon the idea of controlling the runners through the summer, know much about it, I believe it is supposed to be a good idea to leave the grass on the lawn where it falls as it is cut.

Is it all right to mulch with apples? Well, I have heard that they are too acid if used in great quantity. When I make apple sauce, I of course throw the peelings on the garden, and don't jump on me for paring the apples before cooking; I know you're supposed to stew them with the peel on, then strain. But I don't much care for strained apple sauce and I don't like the job of straining, so I peel the apples, then use honey instead of sugar to sustain both my health and virtue. Not to mention that to us the sauce tastes better sweetened with honey.

How often do you put on mulch? Whenever you see a spot that needs it. If weeds begin to peep through any-let them alone until the following spring. Then, after picking the crop, thin the bed again, and repeat this year after year. I have never done this but I certainly would give it a fair trial before I chose either one of the other alternatives I mentioned. Or you can, of course, just promise yourself that you will reform and will do better next time, but broken vows, even those made exclusively to oneself, can be rather uncomfortable to live with.

People ask what to use for mulch. Hay, straw, leaves, pine needles, sawdust, weeds, garbage—any vegetable matter that rots.

Don't some leaves decay too slowly? No, they just remain mulch longer, which cuts down labor. Don't they mat down? If so it doesn't matter, since they are between the rows of growing things and not on top of them. Can one use leaves without hay? Yes, but a combination of the two is better, I think.

Shouldn't the hay be chopped? Don't you have a terrible time spreading long hay? Well, I don't have mine chopped and I don't have a terrible time, and I'm seventy-six and no stronger than the average.

Can you use grass clippings? Yes, but unless you have a huge lawn, they don't go very far. Anyway, although I don't where, just toss an armful of hay on them.

What time of year do you start to mulch? The answer is NOW, whatever the date may be, or at least begin to gather your material. At the *very* least give the matter constructive thought at once; make plans. If you are intending to use leaves, you will unfortunately have to wait until they fall, but you can be prepared to make use of them the moment they drop.

Here is a question I received from Kentucky: "Where can I get salt hay? No one around here ever heard of it." I can only say to that sort of question: if nobody in your community ever heard of some special kind of mulch, you probably can't get that kind; settle for some other.

Many ask: shall I spread manure and plow it under and then mulch? Yes, if your soil isn't very rich; otherwise, mulch alone will answer the purpose.

Over and over: doesn't mulch attract moles, mice, slugs, rats, snakes? In my garden it hasn't, but I'll have more to say about that in the chapter on pests. I got one letter that asked if mosquitoes didn't "hide under the hay, ready to jump out at you when you walk into your garden." Well, ours don't; we have brave mosquitoes which don't bother to hide; they jump at us no matter where we walk.

. . . . . I got one letter that asked if mosquitoes didn't "hide under the hay, ready to jump out at you when you walk into your garden." Well, ours don't; we have brave mosquitoes which don't bother to hide, they jump at us no matter where we walk.

I get letters complaining that mulch won't kill cockleburs, morning glories, witch grass, vetch. I could add that neither will it plant your seeds nor harvest your crops: I am only saying in a sarcastic, friendly way that just because mulch does one hundred things for you, should it be expected to do one hundred and one? However, I do now have reason to hope that one can kill the above menaces with it, and I will tell about this, as far as I have had a chance to try it, in Chapter VIII.

When shall I put on lime, and how much, and should it be put on top of the hay or under it? There are three questions here, and the first two have nothing to do with mulching, and I'm only a mulch expert, not a lime or acid soil one. You proceed with that problem as you did before you ever heard of my system; you can have your soil tested through your agricultural agent. I have, however, heard it said (and not by a fanatic) that my way of gardening may automatically take care of the problem of an acid soil.

As to the third question, you can either put it right in the dirt as you plant, or on top of the mulch, if you do it at a time of year when you can reasonably expect rain or snow to wash it through the mulch by the time the soil should have it. I haven't used any lime for five years and things are doing all right.

How far apart are the rows? Exactly the same distance as if you weren't mulching—that is, when you begin to use my method. However, after you have mulched for a few years your soil will become so rich from rotting vegetable matter that you can plant much more closely than one dares to in the old-fashioned way of gardening.

Here is a rather peculiar question, and I'm not quite sure that I understand it, but since a number of people have asked it, I'll include it: Don't you have to clear a large space in transplanting such things as lettuce and cabbage, so that the plant leaves can spread? Even though I am not perfectly sure about what is meant here, the answer is No. You barely pull the mulch back, put in the plant, and tuck the mulch cozily right up to it, under the spreading leaves, to prevent weeds and hold in moisture.

Doesn't a lot of mulch on flower beds make mounds out of them? No, it doesn't, but don't ask me why. I only know that my heavily-mulched beds are even with the lawn.

Doesn't mulching look awful? Well, there are a lot of answers to that question, and they depend largely on the mulcher—that is, how much he cares about having it look attractive. It doesn't have to look bad. And I could come back with another question: Doesn't a weedy or sun-baked garden look awful? Or I could be a little flippant and say: "Handsome is as handsome does." In the chapter about flowers I will have something more constructive to say about this.

How long does the mulch last? That depends on the kind you use. Try always to have some in reserve, so that it can be replenished as needed.

What is spoiled hay? It's hay that for some reason isn't good enough to feed livestock. It may have, for instance, become moldy—if it was moist when put in the hay mow—but it is just as effective for mulching as good hay and a great deal cheaper.

Is it worthwhile to mulch a city garden? I don't quite see why anyone asks that; I've had no experience with gardening in a town but I've read that mulch is particularly beneficial in the city because it keeps the soot away from the soil. On the other hand, why wouldn't rain wash the soot through the mulch into the soil? Page the experts!

Speaking of making guesses, as I write this book I look over the articles I've written for various periodicals during the years since my first book came out, hoping to find some words of wisdom. I have, here, one written in 1955; some editors, I remember, persuaded me to advise gardeners how to proceed if they suddenly became prophets and knew they were facing a long serious drought.

I have no intention of admitting how many things I said in that article which weren't based on experience; in fact

I don't know how many. Anyway, how could any of it be
based on first-hand knowledge since we never actually know
that a serious drought is ahead of us? Here is just one little
gem I find: "I would plant Butternut squash rather than
Blue Hubbard, although I prefer the latter to all others."
I suppose I said this because Butternut is a small squash
and I no doubt figured that it had a better chance of
maturing than the larger one. However, three years ago we
had a four-months' drought, I planted both Butternut and
Blue Hubbard (not knowing, naturally, of the dry spell we
were in for), and although the former did all right, the
latter really had a heyday. I don't remember how many of
them, weighing between thirty and forty pounds, I gave
away that fall; I kept the prize winner—a fifty-one pound
beauty.

The only excuse I can make for having written the
kind of garden advice I don't believe in—that is, holding
forth about things outside of one's experience—is that I
wasn't arbitrary about it. I didn't, for instance, say that one
must not grow Blue Hubbard in time of drought; I just
said that I thought I would settle for Butternut. Cautious
enough, and possibly even fair.

Now for the million-dollar question: where do you get
mulch? That's difficult to answer but I can say this: if
enough people in any community demand it, I believe that
someone will be eager to supply it. At least that's what
happened within a distance of a hundred miles or so of us
and within a year after my book came out anyone in that
radius could get all the spoiled hay he wanted at sixty-five
cents a bale. If you belong to a garden club, why can't you
all get together and create a demand for spoiled hay? If you
don't belong to a group, you probably at least know quite a
few people who garden and who would be pleased to join
the project.

Use all the leaves around. Clip your cornstalks into
foot-length pieces and use them. Utilize your garbage, tops
of perennials, any and all vegetable matter that rots. In

many localities the utility companies grind up the branches which they cut off when they clear the wires, and often they are glad to dump them near your garden, with no charge. But hurry up before they find out that there is a big demand for them and they decide to make a fast buck. These wood chips make a splendid mulch; I suggest you just ignore anyone who tells you they are too acid.

Recently a man reproached me for making spoiled hay so popular that he can no longer get it for nothing. The important fact, however, is that it has become available and is relatively cheap. The other day a neighbor said to me: "Doesn't it make you feel good to see the piles of hay in so many yards, when you drive around?"

It does; it makes me feel fine.

Now and then I am asked (usually by an irritated expert) why I think I invented mulching. Well, naturally, I don't think so; God invented it simply by deciding to have the leaves fall off the trees once a year. I don't even think that I'm the first, or only person, who thought up my particular variety of all-year-round mulching, but apparently I'm the first to make a big noise about it—writing, talking, demonstrating. And since, in this process of spreading the great news, I have run across many thousands who never heard of the method, and a few hundreds who think it is insane and can't possibly work, and only two people who had already tried it, is it surprising that I have carelessly fallen into the bad habit of sounding as though I thought I originated it?

But why should we care who invented it? Dick Clemence works hard trying to get people to call it the Stout System, which is good because it should have some sort of a short name for people to use when they refer to it, instead of having to tell the whole story each time.

I suppose it does more or less give me a feeling of importance when I come across an article mentioning the Stout System, yet I am cheated out of the full value of that sensation because I've never been able really to identify the whole thing with that little girl who was certainly going to be great and famous some day. What a disgusted look she would have given anyone who would have offered her the title of renowned mulcher!

And it borders on the unenthralling to have the conversation at social gatherings turn to slugs and cabbage worms the minute I show up. And if some professor of psychology, giving an association of ideas' test to a bunch of gardeners, should say "moldy hay" or "garbage," I'm afraid that some of them would come out with "Ruth Stout." Would anyone like that?

What a disgusted look she would have given anyone who would have offered her the title of renowned mulcher!

2

Asparagus—the easiest vegetable of all

One row of our asparagus, fifty feet long, is thirty years old; the other is in its middle twenties. A farmer, who lives not far from us and who grows asparagus commercially, says ours looks very good for its age. He almost promises that it will outlive Fred and me, but he doesn't know much about our sensible diet: raw honey in place of sugar, cereal and bread good enough even for rats and weevils, and a minimum of poisoned foodstuff.

Offhand, I would say there are only two kinds of gardeners who shouldn't grow asparagus: those who don't like it and those who are able to spend only the weekends in the country. As you probably know, it must be gathered every day, and if you aren't around to do that, and if you haven't a neighbor who would be willing to harvest it, take perhaps half of it for himself, and freeze the rest for you, it would hardly do you enough good to be worth it.

But if you like it, it seems a pity not to have your own. For one thing, it gives you something fresh and green early in the spring when you are especially glad to eat almost any food which has just been picked. For another, if you follow my system of caring for it, there's no vegetable which requires less work year after year. For still another, in my thirty years' experience with it, there hasn't been a season when it failed us.

I won't take the time now to stop and cogitate, but I don't believe that last claim can be made for any other vegetable; all others seem to suffer from diseases, or insects, or frost, or too much or too little rain, or woodchucks, or just plain temperament, more than asparagus does. And if you take exception to the last-named drawback, here is a story:

About five years ago, when visitors first began to flock here to see my gardening method, my peppers misbehaved; the plants looked all right—normally green and healthy—but there were no peppers on them. Any expert would glibly tell you the reason for that: soil too rich, which makes a hearty plant but no fruit.

However, all of my visitors reported this same experience that season, and I concluded that everybody's soil could hardly have chosen the same year to be too rich, so, puzzled, I wrote and asked Mr. Warren, of Joseph Harris & Co. what was going on. He replied: "That is the way peppers are behaving this season." No explanation, no apology.

And why should anyone apologize for the behavior of peppers? If some observant child should ask his mother why she was shortening or lengthening the hems of her dresses, what answer could she give him beyond: "That's the way women are behaving this year." And yet they, unlike peppers, have a brain which is presumably to be used for thinking for themselves.

While I'm on the subject I believe I will tell of another even more puzzling performance of peppers. Vaguely I can understand that some seasons they will do better than others, and sometimes I may even think I know why. But this past summer they had me baffled; some of the plants were loaded with peppers (as they have been every year except two of the eighteen that I have been mulching), while others didn't have a single pepper on them. They were all the same variety, were planted at the same time, had received identical treatment, and all looked healthy. I wouldn't have been greatly surprised if some of them had produced considerably better than others, although that had never been the case, but this drastic difference was quite beyond me.

Let's go back to the asparagus bed. If you are going to start one, you will probably use roots, not seeds. I just now looked in the *Garden Encyclopedia* to see what they had to say on the subject, and found, to my surprise, that they recommend one-year-roots rather than two-year-olds. I then turned to my favorite seed catalog (Joseph Harris & Co. Rochester, N. Y.) and saw that they are now selling only one-year asparagus roots, which seems to about settle that question; at least, it would for me if I were planning to start a bed.

Now how should you plant the roots? Thirty years ago I dug trenches for mine, two feet deep and twenty-two inches wide. This was before I began to question (not to say mistrust) the authorities. Today, from advice given by everybody from garden encyclopedias to commercial growers, the trench is getting more and more shallow, until we come to J. A. Eliot who tells us to put the roots at the surface "where all plants belong." He explains why, too, in his little leaflet called "Every garden can easily have asparagus." I would like to put everything he says here in this chapter, but in the first place his leaflet is copyrighted, and in the second, why should I do him out of a half a dollar? He will no doubt mail you a copy if you send him fifty cents. J. A. Eliot, Route 1, Califon, New Jersey.

Anybody who has seen the way asparagus shows up all around the yard and meadow, where birds have apparently dropped seeds, and have seen how it thrives when "planted" thus, on top of the ground, might easily be convinced that surface planting is at least adequate, if not even preferable. I have one row planted that way; I don't remember how I found out that this was permissible.

However, some man in Texas, who read my book which tells about this, wrote me a long explosive letter, saying that this procedure "burnt him so up" that he had to tell me what a terrible mistake it was. A trench should be dug, he said, at least two and one-half feet deep and wide enough for a broad man to walk in without touching either side. The effect, he said, was that of very long graves. He continued with a detailed explanation of how one must fill up this "grave" with dirt and manure and I don't remember what all.

His letter was a prolonged and earnest effort and certainly deserved an answer of some kind, but I didn't know what to say to him. So I sent the letter to Mr. Eliot, and sent Mr. Eliot's leaflet to him, deciding to let them fight it out. If they had lived closer to each other, say in adjoining states, I might not have taken a chance, but with one in New Jersey and the other in Texas I felt that it was unlikely that they would wind up in two of those "very long graves."

I don't want to give away any of Mr. Eliot's good ideas except to mention this: he suggests that we combine flowers and vegetables and tells us why and how. Actually, he hardly needs to explain the suggestion; the moment you hear of it you realize what an excellent idea it is.

And now that we have approved of Mr. Eliot, shall we have some fun disapproving of practically everyone else? For instance, some authorities will tell you to plant a cover crop of soy beans, which is unnecessary work, so we'll ignore it. Others say that manure should be spread over an asparagus bed every fall. Well, if you have some handy, and it didn't cost you anything, go ahead and spread it around if you want to, but if you're using my method of a deep year-round mulch, you don't need it.

Some gardeners put salt on their asparagus bed to do away with the weeds, and I've been told that it does do the trick, but, again, you don't need it if you are mulching with hay. And mulch of course does other things for you besides keeping the weeds down.

You will probably be told that you should cut down the stalks in the autumn and some people will advise you to take them off and burn them. I suggest that you do neither of these things; if you leave them where they are, they will, like everything else, die when their time comes; why not let them rest in peace? They will make their small contribution to the mulch, and if you don't want their seeds to sprout (some gardeners don't) you have little to worry about if the mulch is deep enough.

We will just skip the fantastic idea of making mounds

over the asparagus in order to bleach it; that's for the birds —and some Europeans who were brought up on white asparagus and haven't recovered. These days health-conscious people urge us to eat green-colored food, the greener the better. Assuming that this is a beneficial thing to do isn't it a break that for once the thing that has a lot of nutritive value is less work than that which hasn't?

I have read that it's desirable to mulch an asparagus bed lightly in late autumn to protect the crowns, but that then, in spring, we must remove the covering and cultivate the soil, for what purpose we are left to try to figure out for ourselves. It can't be to soften the soil, or to kill weeds, because under an adequate mulch the earth is always friable and there are no weeds. Once again, my suspicion is that the experts don't know of any good reason why this should be done; too often they behave like a phonograph record that is stuck and goes on and on, getting nowhere.

As you must have guessed by now, about all I do for asparagus is to keep it constantly mulched with loose hay. Baled hay may be too compact to allow the spears to come up through it, and leaves may pack, like a blanket, and therefore have the same drawback. In the fall, I do put a few leaves on the bed (like the experts I don't exactly know why), then a scattering of woodchips, then a good eight inches of loose hay. All this on top of last year's mulch which is rotting effectively by that time.

When I broadcast cotton seed meal over the entire garden in the middle of winter (I will tell about that later) I include the asparagus bed. And once about every three or four years I find myself wondering if the scientists just could be right in claiming that asparagus needs some lime now and then. Usually I think of this when I have a surplus of woodashes and can't decide what to do with them. Then, as likely as not, I scatter some around on the asparagus rows, and I have no idea whether they help, or hinder, or neither; so far they haven't made any noticeable difference in any direction.

It is true, as some detractors like to point out, that mulch prevents the soil from warming up in the spring as rapidly as it would if the ground were bare. This means that your asparagus season will start a little later than it otherwise would, and also means, then, that it lasts farther into the summer. For us this is somewhat of an advantage, for we get occasional frosts right up to the end of May, and sometimes two or three in June, which kill any exposed asparagus stalks. So I'm well pleased to have the crop somewhat delayed.

If, however, for any reason you are in a hurry for asparagus (perhaps you sell it and want it to mature early, when it brings top prices, or perhaps you are merely eager to eat something fresh and green from your garden), there's nothing against pulling the hay away and leaving it off until the ground warms up. That would mean some extra work, and don't forget that you must put the mulch back before weeds get ahead of you. Like many things, it depends on how high a price you are willing to pay. Or you could skip adding to the mulch in the autumn; just see that the hay is there handy, so it won't be much of a job to add mulch in the busy spring.

A still better idea, perhaps, would be to expose only a part of the bed to the sun. This would prolong the season by a week or two; you would harvest the uncovered half first, and the covered part later, during the latter part of the cutting season. Incidentally, I usually try to avoid that word "cutting." Using a tool or knife to gather asparagus is a slow, laborious, inefficient method as compared to just snapping off the tender part of the stalk. Some people object to this because they don't like the looks of the broken-off stalks. Well, I guess that any esthetic objection to anything is unarguable, but remember, you have to put up with this particular unsightliness for only seven or eight weeks, then the asparagus bed becomes a mass of attractive ferns and the broken stalks are no longer visible.

When we contemplate buying something we usually ask

the price of it, then decide whether or not it is worth that much to us. But when we expend time and energy we often just go ahead and pay, not stopping to ask if the objective justifies our actions. If we are over-tired and cranky at the end of a day we might pause and ask ourselves: what did I do today to get myself into this state, and was it worth it to anyone, including me? Since you wound up being cross and irritable the answer may well be No, but how about the criticism you might get from some member of your family or the neighbors if you had neglected to do this or that? And now I'm lost, for I've never been able to get to the bottom of what goes on in the minds of people who order their lives (including their asparagus beds) by other people's standards.

Not only for asparagus, but for the whole garden, hay is the best mulch of all, according to J. A. Eliot. He says that for nutritive value it is superior to manure and his reasoning goes like this: part of the nutrients in the hay which is fed to horses and cows go to build up the body of the animals and to make milk; manure is the residue. But a rotting hay mulch has all of these nutrients left in it. That sounds logical to me.

I planted my asparagus long before I began the year-round-mulching method and therefore the rows are four feet apart, which is farther than they need to be. After you have mulched for a few years, you are able to plant things closer together, I have found.

This space between my two rows of asparagus isn't entirely wasted; early vegetables—lettuce, onions, spinach—may be planted there, and also summer lettuce. I have read of all sorts of performances that people go through to shade lettuce in hot weather; asparagus, when its harvesting season is over, seems to do this adequately.

Somebody told me that lima beans do better with a little shade, and since there's no sense in just automatically disbelieving everything one hears, I tried this last summer, planting some limas between the asparagus rows. In that one trial (which proves, I guess, exactly nothing) I found the idea unsatisfactory; the bean leaves did stay green longer, and the asparagus protected the bushes from the early light frosts, but I got more than twice as many beans from the row I planted in full sunlight. As I say, one trial means very little, but I doubt if I will have the enterprise to do that again.

Later, if you keep on reading, you will come to some unfriendly remarks about compost piles. One advantage of them is that you have, right there, for the taking, a bushel or so of excellent dirt to perhaps use in planting a rosebush, or to give to someone. Well, my whole garden is covered with this wonderful commodity, and the simplest, handiest place to get some of it is between the rows of asparagus, as easy as taking it from a compost pile.

I really believe I could get away with planting squash and pumpkin between the rows of asparagus; they would be shaded for only a short time, because soon the vines are roaming around everywhere, and the leaves would get all the sun they needed as soon as they reached beyond the boundaries of that relatively narrow enclosure.

This spring I had an inspiration about pole beans, and apparently it's going to work. Last summer the Blue Hubbard squash vines crawled all over my asparagus; in several instances a twenty or thirty pound squash hung suspended, bending the asparagus stalks over, making them look like tired old men, but not breaking them. Why couldn't one plant pole beans close by a particularly thick stalk of asparagus and give them support in that way instead of all that business of putting in poles? One could, and I did, and the beans are running up the stalks.

Since that stalk supported a heavy squash, it could surely have handled a bumper crop of beans. Even if it bent over, it still would keep the beans off the ground. Among other drawbacks about poles, aside from having to cut them and put them in the ground, mine are usually on the anemic side and often break when they are heavy with beans. This past year an added disadvantage was that when they broke they landed on some tomatoes which already had enough to contend with—too much rain, not enough sun, and some kind of an animal taking bites out of them.

If I didn't have an asparagus bed I would be tempted to follow Mr. Eliot's suggestion: plant it here and there in combination with flowers. And even if I were a genius at landscape gardening I wouldn't tell you any of my valuable

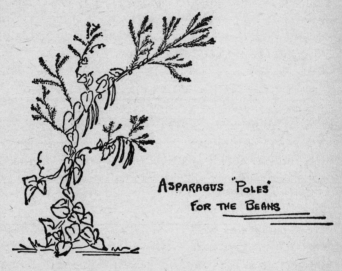

ASPARAGUS "POLES" FOR THE BEANS

. . . Why couldn't one plant pole beans close by a particularly thick stalk of asparagus and give them support in that way instead of all that business of putting in poles?

ideas about combining flowers and vegetables in a bed; you would enjoy the whole thing more if you thought up your own.

But I find I can't resist making one suggestion: why not plant asparagus in the tulip bed? The flowers will be on the way out and their leaves will begin to die and look ugly just about the time asparagus turns into an attractive fern. And think what fun it would be to "tiptoe through the tulips" to gather your asparagus!

3

Some startling things about corn and some comments on beans, peas and squash

I have learned a few things about corn during the past five years but I am first going to tell about something I've tried without success; I failed because I didn't do as I was told, and with that dismal background I might just skip the whole thing, except that the idea is most valuable to anyone who wants to grow his own corn but has limited space.

Most Americans love corn-on-the-cob, and many of them know from experience that its flavor deteriorates rapidly after it has been picked. Therefore, most people with a bit of ground available would like very much to grow their own.

Taking into consideration the size of your family and the approximate number of ears of corn each one would probably consume in a week, then adding a certain amount for guests and perhaps some for freezing, it's easy to figure how much to plant. For instance, if by this process of arithmetic you find that you will want sixty ears a week for, let us say, eight weeks, and if in your experience you can count on three ears for every two stalks, you will need three hundred and twenty stalks. And if you plant them in the orthodox way, in rows three feet apart and one foot apart in the row, you will need a piece of ground forty feet long and twelve feet wide, which is more space than many people can spare for one vegetable, even corn.

You don't need nearly that much space to grow corn, Dick tells us, and along with this welcome news I will now introduce him properly. In January of 1959 I read an article in *Organic Gardening & Farming* by Professor Richard V. Clemence; the short blurb about him explained that he was Chairman of the Economics Department at Welles-ley College, where he had been teaching for ten years.

The article was called "Eleven Ways to Make Mulch Work." He had been a year-round mulcher for some time, long before he had ever heard of me, but he generously gave me honorable mention instead of barking: "What makes that woman think she invented mulch?"

I wrote and asked him a number of questions, for his "Eleven Ways" included some new and interesting sugges-tions. He answered at length, the correspondence con-tinued, and in July he and his wife and young daughter came to see us. As you may know, it's a risky business to meet someone in person whom you have come to like a good deal just through letters, but this time it came out fine; everybody liked everybody, common interests abounded, and little Melissa and I even discovered that we were both devoted to Erle Stanley Gardner.

The reason I tell all this is because I am going to quote Dr. Clemence abundantly in this chapter and in chapters VIII and XII, and it seemed a good idea for you to have some sort of picture of him, rather than keep saying to your-self: Who the dickens is Dick?

Why do I have so much faith in him? Because he doesn't guess, he reports and in all of his experimenting, as far as I can judge, doesn't care which side wins. His mind isn't made up in advance, his emotions aren't involved, and he is interested only in the truth. But I am exaggerating; since he's human he naturally hopes he's right if he has, for in-stance, a theory about killing witch grass (which he has; keep reading.) But insofar as is humanly possible he has a scientific and detached attitude, and is not out to prove that the "other side" is wrong, not to say ridiculous.

Dick should be collaborating with me on this book and he would be if we lived near enough to each other to make this workable. Failing that, I will pass along as much as I can of what I have learned from him.

In that first article which I read of his he offered the startling information that "Sweet corn spaced six inches each way will do just as well as it will with the rows three feet apart, and you get six times as much corn from the same area." I wrote him that I had never heard of anything so crazy, and that I could hardly wait to try it, adding, however, that my sister, who spends the summers out here, was a corn addict (not to mention me), and was it really safe to plant it that way?

He replied that it was, but that the ground must be very rich, that I had better use a lot of manure. Well, I didn't want to bother to do that, so I compromised by planting the corn six inches apart in the row, but spacing the rows a foot apart instead of the half-foot he recommended, and instead of the traditional three feet. That was last summer.

There is no use pretending that I wasn't nervous about the whole thing, and I stayed nervous, because the corn didn't get normally tall and seemed to hesitate unduly about starting to produce ears. By early July I was bordering on the pessimistic about it, comforted only by the fact that Dick was planning to come to see us before long. And although I was very much tempted to at once do some drastic thinning of that bewildered-looking patch, I decided to wait until the cause of it all arrived to look over the situation.

Before that happened, John Lorenz dropped in, had a look around, and bluntly called my attention to the fact that my corn was lousy (not in the literal sense), that it wasn't normally tall, wasn't making ears properly, wasn't green enough. What the hell, he said—I had better get out there and thin it, but I told him that I thought I would wait until Dick came, and would ask him what to do. (John had read Dick's articles).

But when I went to the garden later that day, I decided I didn't dare wait; the corn was certainly getting decidedly yellow, and it looked anemic and ill-treated in general. I did a job of thinning, then scattered some cotton seed meal around, and it rained that night, so I was spared the job of watering in order to get the meal washed down to the soil.

By the time Dick came (a week later) the leaves looked a little greener and promises of ears had begun to show up, but sort of tentatively, as though reserving the right to change their minds and disappear at any moment, if they felt like it.

To make a long-winded story at least a *little* less long, Dick said that we would get some corn, and we did have enough. There was none to freeze, but that wasn't my intention, anyway.

John is against this close-planting method, no matter how rich the soil is, because, he says, the sun can't get to the corn; he doesn't believe it's possible to get a good crop that way. When I reminded him that Dick actually does it, he just shook his head, so, to humor him, I wrote and asked Dick about the shade angle, and he replied:

"The idea that close planting of corn makes it too shady for good growth can hardly have much in it, or my corn would not grow well at all. I should go further and say that a little shade is desirable for corn and almost everything else. During most of the growing season, the sun is high enough in the sky to afford light from above for the whole garden anyway. I have grown excellent corn right in the shade of a tree, where it got very little direct sunlight."

Did you ever sit and listen to two people argue about something, with each of them convinced, at the outset, that he was right? I expect you have; few people have escaped that experience. If the arguers are reasonable, intelligent people, they will start out saying sensible things and using their minds to make their points. But often, as they continue, each realizing that he hasn't made the slightest dent in the other's armor (that is, that the other is as blind and pig-headed as he is, although he wouldn't put it exactly that way), the mind sort of recedes into the background and the emotions take over; presently not much that either of them says makes sense, they will startle you with the "facts" they present, and will finally wind up calling each other's remarks stupid and ridiculous.

Yet I have actually discovered, when on occasion I have listened carefully through some long heated argument, that the antagonists are really in agreement but don't realize it. Also, if you want to take the trouble, you can sometimes even show them that this is true, unless they are too annoyed by now to do anything but gulp down another drink and glare at each other.

If Dick and John should get together, though, I don't think the talk would get out of hand. All Dick has to say is that he is speaking from actual experience. My reason for wanting them to discuss the thing is that I want John to be convinced.

In the meantime I'm not going to plant corn that close again because I don't want to bother with manure. However, I would certainly use it and plant Dick's way if I didn't have the space to grow corn farther apart. This year I put the rows two feet apart and spaced the corn eight inches apart in the row. It came out all right.

Although I have a few acres available, I keep my garden as small as possible, to cut down the labor. It's surprising how many people, once having started a garden bigger than they need, can't stand to abandon any part of it. I'm glad that I too went through that phase which lasted with me for a number of years, otherwise it would be difficult for me to understand how people can keep on working harder than they would like to (and even, perhaps, than they should) on a garden bigger than they need.

Sometime ago, when I was giving a talk to a large community group, we all got almost hysterical during the question period because I simply couldn't bear the thought of one of the men having an admittedly unnecessarily big garden and I kept returning to him and trying to convert him. But I'm not going to attempt to say anything now which might make anyone mend his ways in this respect; I guess it's like religion: you will either see the light or you won't, and you will just have to take the consequences until you do.

I will only point out that my garden is 50 x 40 (this includes two rows of asparagus, one of strawberries and one of raspberries) and feeds three people for seven months, and two of us all year, and many guests. And if I could make up my mind which squash I like best, I wouldn't need that much space. Since my soil has become so rich from rotting mulch, I have a few other space-saving tricks besides planting everything much more closely than I used to. For instance, I put bush peas, both edible pod and regular, between the rows of corn, and this works very well with the corn rows only two feet apart, because I am careful to keep the peas standing upright by propping them well with baled hay.

When I pick corn I take the clippers along and cut the finished stalks in short pieces and leave it all lying there to rot. And the roots are left in the ground. Of course Dick comes up with a good scheme about corn stalks which he calls "nearly ideal," and which you will find in Chapter VIII.

Last spring I also tried his way of simply sticking each grain of corn in the ground in planting; after first marking the row with a string, I knelt down and pushed each kernel of corn down through the mulch into the soft earth with my fingers. Dick says you can plant this way only if the mulch is thin, otherwise it is too difficult to get the kernels into the soil.

This means that the corn comes up right through the hay; which has some advantages: the ground stays soft and moist and the weeds are defeated. Also, crows ignore corn which is either planted this way or which has hay thrown on top of it immediately after it's planted; I haven't been able to figure out any reason for this, but I will bet that any armchair gardener could tell us.

Many of the visitors to my patch have been surprised that corn planted so shallowly, and not hilled up, isn't blown over by the wind. Mine used to be before I began to mulch, but not anymore. I never did make mounds around corn, but I planted it more deeply in pre-mulching days. One recent caller had a theory why hilled-up corn blows over and mine doesn't, but I seem to be somewhat allergic to theories and I've forgotten what he said, although I did find it interesting.

Quite a number of growers (here in Connecticut, at least) have trouble with animals getting their corn just about two days before it's ready to be picked. It seems that raccoons, squirrels, woodchucks and skunks are the offenders, and even a fence is no help against raccoons and squirrels.

. . . . . . *Quite a number of growers have trouble with animals getting their corn just about two days before it's ready to be picked; it seems that raccoons, squirrels, woodchucks and skunks are the offenders, and even a fence is no help against raccoons and squirrels.*

I have solved this problem, and how I ever got the idea in the first place that it would work, I can't imagine, but it has saved my corn for many years. When a row is about ready to eat I prop old screens (window, door, fire—any kind) up against the stalks; if I haven't enough of the screens I fill the gaps with bushel baskets and any other obstacles I can scrape up.

One might guess that my barricade has nothing to do with it, that the animals just haven't got around to my corn for some reason; to settle that question I have left a few ears unprotected each time, and usually those have been attacked. And if anyone wants further proof here it is: this past summer I didn't get the screens placed in time, and one fine morning I found the entire first row of stalks pulled down and the ears gnawed. From then on I put the barricade up for each row and had no more trouble.

Then, two seasons ago, the raccoons somehow figured out how to outwit that project. So I put small paper bags over the almost-mature ears, fastening them with rubber bands. That worked for only a few nights. Next, I used the paper cartons that orange juice comes in, and tin cans open at both ends. In no time at all the animals had that licked. Finally, I took ten-foot lengths of hardware cloth, about ten inches wide, and fastened them with twisters along both sides of a row of corn, right over the ears. This worked; the animals couldn't get the corn, the catch being that I couldn't either without spending about an hour to pick eight or nine ears.

I spent the following winter cogitating. Both my sister and I are very fond of corn; was I able and willing to devote my declining years to fighting for something that was rightfully mine? The answer came out "No."

The solution was obvious and I told several men gardeners that I was planning to put up a corn cage (inside my garden plot) about 20 by 30 feet and 7 or 8 feet high, with a wire roof on it. I could also, I decided, plant raspberry bushes in a section of it, thus defeating birds, for although I am fond of the latter (aren't we all?), I can love them a little more if they aren't feasting on some of my produce.

Each man I spoke to had a different idea about the corn cage, and I got more and more bewildered. Finally, I asked my brother Rex's advice, and he took complete charge— planning the whole thing, then ordering the material, then bringing his gardener and another man over here to help build it. They mixed concrete, put up steel poles, used turn-buckles (whatever they may be), and the finished contraption is really magnificent. If any raccoon can figure out how to get an ear of my corn now, I will admire his ingenuity so much that I won't begrudge it to him.

True, the cage cost quite a little (a few hundred dollars), but perhaps you could do the work yourself, thus doing away with at least some of the expense.

I guess you will agree that no one seems to approve of the way the other fellow spends his money, so when anyone says to me (obviously in criticism): "Did you really spend hundreds of dollars on *that*?" I in turn ask *him* a question: "Would you spend a few hundred dollars on a trip somewhere?" And when he usually says yes to that, I reply:

"Well, bon voyage! You'll come home after a month or so and then what have you got but memories? Meanwhile, for the rest of my life I'll be eating my own freshly picked corn every summer and for memories I can use the one time I went abroad even if it was forty years ago. Also, I don't like to travel and I am too busy to fool around with memories."

When I strongly approve of something, I am likely to spread that news; ever since I first grew Joseph Harris' *Wonderful* corn. I've had a good deal to say for it. Other corn fanatics who read my comments about *Wonderful* but remain loyal to their own favorites, send me samples of theirs to try, but so far I have remained faithful to my own pet for the main crop.

How ardent and articulate most people are when talking about something they wholly believe in, from a Great Cause to a variety of bean! If somebody could only figure out what the "right" thing is for humanity, then get a reasonable number of people to honestly believe it, we might— But there's no use in dreaming up nonsense; the rest of us wouldn't listen, we would just call the others names, such as faddists and fanatics.

Speaking of enthusiasm, I am thinking of a man named Oliver Griffith, who sent me some wonderful beans. But, what with one thing and another, I forgot who had given them to me, so I couldn't write and report on them. Two years later I went to Columbus, Ohio, to give a talk at the annual state convention of the *Natural Food Associates*, and shortly after I got there, a man walked up to me and demanded, without any pretense of leading up to the subject:

"Did you eat my beans?"

I won't try to tell you how amusing Mr. Griffith was during the whole two days of the convention, popping up every now and then to make funny remarks on numerous subjects including, just often enough, beans. He told me that he didn't know what variety those were that he sent me; he saves his own seed. I did my best to convince him that I have no talent as a seed-saver, so he said he would send me some each year, and I think he will.

If he hadn't already won me over, I would have succumbed when he told me that he keeps a copy of my first garden book in the waiting room of his beauty parlor, there in Columbus, and when someone helps himself to the book, or when it gets shabby, he replaces it. The name of his place is the Marcella Beauty Shop, and you really should take a trip to Columbus and have your hair done and maybe steal a book.

For many years I have planted Bansei edible soy beans, the only kind I knew about. Then, about two years ago, a woman in Pennsylvania sent me some of another variety and I planted them and found them far superior to Bansei. They had a better flavor, stayed green considerably longer, and were almost twice as large. We think soy beans are at their best when they are fresh and green, but the season for eating Bansei at this stage is much too short unless you make several plantings, which seems a nuisance to me. Also, the small size of Bansei makes them something of a trial to prepare.

I wrote and asked this woman where I could get these beans, and received the answer I was afraid I would get: I couldn't buy them; the firm she had originally got them from wasn't in business any longer. So, bribing her with a copy of another book I had written (not about gardening) I succeeded in getting her to send me all the seeds she could spare, and I promised her to try to get some commercial grower to carry them. I of course first tried Carl Warren, but he told me that he and Joe Harris didn't like soy beans. Of all things! Then I wrote to Billy Hepler Seed Co., 76 Madbury Road, Durham, New Hampshire, and they said they would grow them. They are listed in his catalog under the original name: *Giant Green* soy bean.

Like corn, beans can be planted by pushing them one by one into the soil through the mulch, which is a quick practical way to do it, if you are putting them around a pole or around asparagus. But if you want to plant some bush beans, to have while you are waiting for the pole variety to mature, I find it better to pull the mulch back a little and make a drill and plant, then cover with hay.

I'm afraid I always plant bush beans too thick, and it just occurred to me that I could cure myself of that bad habit if I pushed them individually through the hay. I have also been thinking that if you want to find out what your faults and drawbacks are in any activity you engage in, write a book about it.

Peas, another seed that may be covered with hay as soon as planted, differ in one respect from corn and beans. Because it is necessary to get peas in early, something should be done about thawing the ground for them; this entails no extra work, the only thing required is knowing in advance where you are going to put them.

If you decide this in the fall, you could avoid putting on added mulch in that section, when you may be spreading some over the rest of the garden. At any rate, you will certainly know by early March where you are going to plant your peas, and it's wise to rake the mulch away from that area a few weeks in advance, and let the sun thaw and warm the soil.

This will perhaps be the spot where you will plant corn later, so, now, when you replace the mulch, you can leave it thin enough to keep the corn planting as easy a job as possible. If you should yield to the temptation to leave the mulch off entirely until after the corn is planted, you will probably be sorry; if you have much rain weeds will abound, and if you should get a dry spell the soil will be sunbaked. One thing I found out the hard way in that pre-mulch era was that corn seeds will flatly refuse to co-operate if you put them in a dry soil, which stays dry.

Although I have tried many varieties of peas, the only ones I have had real luck with are *Lincoln*. A great many people have had this same experience, so I am glad to give *Lincoln* another plug, which I have often done in the past.

The only other seeds I can think of which may be covered with hay immediately after planting are sweetpeas and squash; no doubt there are others. I suppose it's safe to say that all big seeds will stand it and, for all we know, may also like it.

Although Blue Hubbard squash is still my favorite, partly on account of its beauty, I have recently come to like Buttercup very much. And for the past two seasons I've been growing Baby Butternut and Baby Blue Hubbard in addition to the regular full-size ones.

. . . . But in spite of my devotion to Blue Hubbard, I don't intend to let it get away with murder, as it usually does. This year the squash killed the promising Sugar Baby watermelon vines by wandering all over them.

But in spite of my devotion to Blue Hubbard, I don't intend to let it get away with murder any more, as it usually does. This year the squash killed the promising Sugar Baby watermelon vines by wandering all over them.

However blessed you may be with imagination, and whatever may have been your many years of experience, it seems impossible, when you put in hills of squash in spring, for you to be able to visualize how far they will probably wander before frost. This past season, due to my experiment with the close planting of corn, I had more space than usual and allotted it to Blue Hubbard; I figured out where to put the hills of watermelon and felt sure they were safe. Well, they weren't.

I have always felt that I can to a large extent (well, to some extent, anyway) control the vines, and early in their life, when I see them heading in the wrong way, I re-direct them. But events of all varieties (not only in the garden) simply pile up too rapidly in the summer, happenings abound, and while I am looking in several other directions, the Blue Hubbard expands in *every* direction.

Some visitor last summer asked me if I pruned squash vines to get more and larger yields; this had never occurred to me, but I decided to do it this year by cutting off all of the vines which are headed in the (to me) wrong direction. Well when the time came, I didn't have the heart; they simply looked too industrious and purposeful. So I let them alone.

I am more indebted to my visitors and readers than I could ever say; more, even, than I can estimate myself. Not only for beans and many other gifts, and for helpful advice, but also for stories which provide a smile.

I got a long letter from a woman (in the South, I think) telling me in detail of all the advantageous things which mulch was doing for her, but she concluded with: "I am worried about my corn. It has weeds all around it because my husband won't let me pull the mulch up close to it; he says it will stop breathing if I do."

Well, could I prove her husband was wrong? No, I couldn't, so I simply wrote and said to tell him that maybe my closely-mulched corn wasn't breathing but it kept producing, year after year, two fine ears on every stalk. And I added: "Maybe corn doesn't have to breathe; maybe it doesn't even want to."

4

Potatoes in the iris bed and onions in the hay

One day, a summer or two ago, some visitors were standing on the edge of my vegetable garden, admiring the potatoes I had planted in my nonchalant fashion, and one of them said:

"I did it this way too. The minute I read your book I went right out and got some Irish Cobblers and threw them on the ground and piled a lot of hay on them."

As the woman spoke she made a sweeping gesture directed at the meadow surrounding our garden which was at the moment covered with tall grass. I was a little startled and exclaimed:

"You didn't plant them in a field like that, did you? In tall grass?"

"Yes, I did," she answered. "Was that wrong?"

"We-ell, I don't know," I said. "What happened?"

"I never had such fine potatoes in my life," she replied.

So apparently it wasn't wrong, and I couldn't resist trying it myself the next day, using potatoes which were meant to be eaten, not planted. The result was a lot of tiny ones; it was too late in the season for them to mature.

In my first book I had only a sentence or two about growing potatoes without covering them with dirt, for at that time I had never tried it. I said that one should make a furrow, drop the potatoes in it, then cover them with hay. I have now found that the furrow is unnecessary.

There is no need to take up space in your vegetable garden for this crop; any sunny spot will answer. I have a large bed of iris which is rather far from the house; the driveway circles around it. When I put the iris there three years ago I left a wide space at the edge, intending to plant day lilies for a border, and I kept the section covered with hay to outwit weeds. However, I didn't get around to putting in the lilies, and last summer I decided this unused space would be satisfactory for potatoes; I tossed some around on the previous year's mulch and covered them with a foot of loose hay.

I may have put on more mulch than was necessary, but I didn't want the sprouts to come through in time to get nipped by a June frost. I had been warned not to cover the plants after they made an appearance. (This is something to remember when you read later what I have to say about witch grass.) Today we are told that whole potatoes are more satisfactory for planting than cut-up ones, but some people, I know, grow theirs from potato peelings.

Are you thinking that iris and potatoes in a bed are an odd combination? Well, I bet that if I could pin you down, you would have to admit that the only thing against it is that it "isn't done." And did you ever stop to think of all the things that weren't "done" until somebody started doing them? You don't have to go back to the pre-historic era, either, to make out an impressive list of them; I need think back no farther than my own childhood.

There were no movies nor TV in those days for us children to sit and watch by the hour. And we didn't ride to school in a bus or car and then go to the gymnasium for some much-needed exercise. Neither did we rot our teeth with soft drinks; the last time I had my teeth cleaned, the dentist suddenly began to laugh and I asked him what was funny.

"Well, it's ridiculous what a kick I get out of cleaning thirty-two teeth all in one mouth," he replied.

But we really don't have to go back to my youth for our list. Twenty, even ten years ago, madmen weren't flying all around throwing poison indiscriminately on insects, bees, birds, fish, children, while others spent their time chasing after the moon.

Compared to all these frenzied activities, putting iris and

potatoes in the same bed seems almost too tame an inno-
vation to deserve mentioning. But I'm not bragging about
it; I didn't do it for effect, only because it was convenient.

Even pictorially I can't see anything against this combination, although you may think I'm saying that just because I want to believe it. While the iris are at their lovely
best, in full bloom, the potato plants have hardly begun to
show. And even if they had, I wouldn't mind; a healthy
potato vine free from bugs (mine never have had any) is
far from unattractive, and if a person didn't recognize it,
he would probably admire it if he was told it was a rare
plant from a far-off land.

In that connection I can't resist telling you about some
rather gushy visitors at my brother Rex's home who asked
the name of the unusual-looking flower in the bouquet in
the living room. Rex gave it some highsounding name or
other (probably Latin), said it was extremely rare, very
difficult to grow, hard to procure, and outlandishly expensive. However, he had, he said, a pull with a certain dealer
in rare plants, and although he could make no promises, he
might be able to get one or two for them.

Eagerly the visitors asked him to try to; to heck with the
expense, if they could just have the prestige of owning this
fascinating flower. Actually the bloom was from one of
Rex's rhubarb plants, which he had allowed to flower, or,
perhaps, had just failed to nip in the bud.

Last summer somebody sent me a clipping of an article
about mulch from the *Ladies Home Journal*. The author,
Richard Pratt, said some kind things about my book, but he
also said that his preoccupation with plants was largely
pictorial, and that therefore I probably wouldn't even want
him as an assistant. I liked the whole piece so much that I
wrote and thanked him for the praise he gave my system
and I offered him a job, not as assistant but as boss of the
pictorial department, provided he wouldn't interfere with
my fine arrangement of iris and potatoes.

I didn't mention that there was no salary (just glory)

connected with the job, deciding to break that news when he showed up for work. Besides, anyone who read my other garden book couldn't fail to realize that I am free from the burden of superfluous possessions and surplus cash; I'm sure this fact leaks out through the pages.

In his friendly answer, he said: "I bet the potato vines make a stunning picture, and what a clever way to cover the iris, and what a painless way to grow potatoes."

Never mind that perhaps he was only being pleasant and didn't mean a word of it. If there's anything more foolhardy than digging down under the surface of a compliment to try to decide whether or not it's sincere, I don't know what it is.

This combination bed never at any time looks so unattractive that I wouldn't want it nearer the house, (and it would follow as the night the day that Fred would call them "iris potatoes"). Iris plants don't look very good after they are through blooming, but ours, with sturdy green potato vines covered with pretty white flowers growing around them, don't look offensive. When, eventually, the

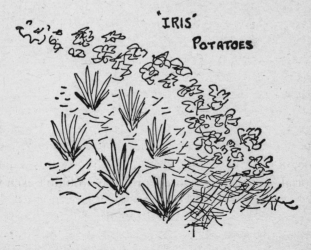

. . . This combination bed never at any time looks so unattractive that I wouldn't want it nearer the house (and it would follow as the night the day that Fred would call them "iris potatoes.")

potato plants, too, begin to die, of course the whole bed is scraggly-looking, but not any more so than the iris alone would be.

However, by now the lady has certainly protested too much; it's high time to drop the pictorial angle.

I would only insult anyone's intelligence by trying to prove how easy it is to plant potatoes my way; that is obvious. About the taste, our own seem better to us than those one buys in market, but that may not mean much; we may be prejudiced. However, for the past several years many people we know have been complaining of the increasingly poor quality of potatoes, and I'm not talking about the so-called food faddists or organically-minded people; I mean the run-of-the-mill person who cheerfully eats many varieties of worthless or worse-than-that junk without giving the matter any thought. And I don't know why they notice the poor quality of the present-day potato when the deficiencies of so many other foods seem to elude them.

One advantage of growing potatoes on top of the ground is that as soon as the blossoms begin to drop off, the hay can be carefully lifted and some small potatoes separated from their stems without hurting the mother plant; then the hay is replaced. Thus we eat "new" potatoes for a longer season than we could if they were planted the old laborious way. Dick Clemence put me up to that trick. (However, I am not going to mention him every time I tell you of one of his ideas, except his more important ones; otherwise, I would feel obliged to call this book "By Benefit of Clemence.")

Of course iris belong in the chapter on flowers, but since they have been brought up, shall we finish with them? My brother Rex is somewhat of an authority on this flower, and by that I don't mean to insult him; without intending to, I have acquired such a reputation for belittling experts, authorities, scientists, that for me to use such a title for anyone seems to amount to calling him a bad name. This, in spite of the fact that I have repeatedly said that I have nothing against authorities as such; I am only in favor of putting a question mark after just about everything they say.

Well, *Popular Gardening* asked me to write an article about Rex's iris, which wasn't hard to do. First I gave him a meal of his favorite food, navy beans boiled with salt pork (this, to put him in a first-class humor, and, besides, it's the easiest dish in the world to prepare). Then I sat with paper and pen and wrote down whatever he said, and later typed it, and still later cashed the check.

At first he gloated: "For twenty-five years I've been hoping you would ask me why I'm so crazy about iris. Now, at last, you want to know."

I assured him that I didn't give a darn, personally, but under the circumstances what could I do but listen?

"I bet you don't even know iris don't like mulch," he went on. "The rhizomes have to be planted practically at the surface of the ground; they need the sun." Then he said: "So shall we drop the whole thing and play Twenty Questions, or something?"

"No, go ahead and bore me," I replied. "Why do you grow so much iris?"

So he continued at some length, and with such enthusiasm and variety that at times he sounded like an extremely clever advertiser and at other times like a poet. When he finished he had made every other flower look pretty dull and inferior, even though he grows, and enjoys, quite a big variety.

He claimed that one doesn't have to spend more than somewhere between seventy-five cents and two dollars for a rhizome, in order to have a "collection of iris glory." And it's easy, he said, to follow the directions which come with every order; iris demand sunshine, good drainage, shallow planting, and soil with a little nourishment in it, but not too much. And that's all.

Then he expanded on the opportunity this flower offers

for playing with color, and I remembered the spot, thirty feet long and three feet wide, which he had devoted, for a couple of years, entirely to blue iris: the extremely delicate Azure Skies at one end, deepening gradually to the somber Black Hills at the other. His Rhapsody in Blue was played by fifteen well-known varieties.

I mentioned this, and Rex said that one could do the same thing with yellows, pinks, reds or blends. And you couldn't even begin to do it with any other flower.

As we said good night to Rex, I asked him when one should separate iris; in other words, when should we drive over for a few bushels of rhizomes?

That was how my bed of iris got started, four years ago. However, don't jump to the conclusion that I am being orthodox about it. I admit that Rex knows a great deal more about gardening than I do and can be relied on when he gives information, although I'm reminded of that day long ago in Kansas (where we were brought up), when the teacher asked him, during the geography lesson, what color the ocean was. He screwed up his face in deep thought and finally came up with: "Well, at night it's a sort of pinkish hue."

I told myself that this could be another time that he was mistaken. I had known for quite a while that all of the experts agreed that iris must be in a sunny spot, and should be separated every now and then. Now I had been told that they wouldn't stand for mulch. Then I pondered over the few clumps of blue iris (two varieties) which grow around our frog pond: they are in full shade, have never been divided, and have been mulched for some ten or twelve years *and* they look healthy and are quite pretty.

Now I don't say they get preferred treatment, and they might be better off if I obeyed the rules. But wouldn't I be worse off—doing all the work of dividing and weeding them?

So I decided to treat the quantities of iris which Rex gave me as I saw fit. The spot I had picked out for them was in full sun; so far, so good. Another happy thought was that Rex had said they should be planted near the surface, and I remembered a letter that a woman (in Maryland, I think it was) had written me, saying that after she had read what I said in my first book about planting potatoes just by throwing hay on them, she tossed a lot of day-lily bulbs around and threw hay on them and they behaved beautifully. So I did that with the iris.

They have bloomed for four years, are spreading normally as far as I can tell, and seem healthy. I did lose about a half-dozen last winter (all one variety), but the weather was severe; many people in this vicinity lost all of their iris (unmulched), so I am certainly not going to blame my loss on the mulching.

When I gave a talk to the Community Center in New Milford a few months ago about my gardening method, someone asked about iris, and I briefly told the above story, ending with: "I don't claim that my way gets the best results, but I do believe one can have a fine showing without any work beyond putting additional hay on the bed each year. However, I've had this bearded iris only four years; I don't know what may happen to them in the future."

What else can we just throw on the ground, expecting it to grow? Crocuses, I should think, because they pop up here and there where they have never been planted. This would indicate that the wind or a bird has carried the seed to that spot, and I suppose it follows that the bulb is there on the surface of the ground.

Some enthusiast asked me if one could treat bulbs in general that way—daffodil, tulip, and so on. I have never tried it, and at the risk of being called a dyed-in-the-wool conservative, I believe I would hesitate to do that to a tulip bulb.

Onion sets respond heartily to this surface treatment which I should have guessed long before I did, since they often merrily sprout in our kitchen bin. I never cared for the job of sticking a whole quart of little onion sets one by one into the ground, and one spring morning a few years ago I said to myself: there must be some way to get around this tedious performance; why not pretend they are potatoes? So I scattered them over the previous year's mulch, tossed some hay on top, had fine onions, and of course have planted them that way ever since. An added advantage is that you can do this as early as you like, not having to wait until the ground thaws.

My guess is that if you would like to have fresh scallions through the summer and don't want to bother to put in seeds, you could keep some sets spread out in a dry place and plant them (or, rather, throw them on the hay) all season long, as you wanted some. I hope I can remember to try that next year.

This whole business of cutting down work in the garden has got to the point where people expect me to constantly come up with new short cuts, but I'm afraid my ingenuity is about to call it a day. However, one can also simplify other fields of activity which I have enlarged on in my last book: *It's A Woman's World.*

One evening in summer a men's garden club came to have a look at my method, and as they stood around inspecting the vegetables and one man after another lifted the mulch and exclaimed over the rich moist earth wriggling with earthworms, I no doubt said over and over, in answer to various questions: "Oh, no, you don't have to bother to do that. Just—"

When the mosquitoes and gathering dusk drove us indoors to finish our discussion, we gathered in the living-room, and I heard one of the men mutter to another: "Look! No rugs down, no curtains at the windows. She evidently doesn't believe in working in the house, either."

I imagine that quite a lot of wives got a colorful report later that evening, and some of them probably were scornful, while a few may have been envious; I'm afraid we can safely bet, though, that not a rug came up and not a curtain came down. My guess is that if our homes weren't quite so "pretty," our faces would, often, be more so; that is, pleasant and relaxed-looking.

If you are wakeful some night, and don't want to take a sleeping pill but don't want to just lie there, either, try to figure this out: why do women spend time and money on their hair, face, and hands, presumably to make themselves attractive, then, as style dictates, wear unbecoming, even outlandish clothes? And when you have that settled, work on this one: why does it occur to so few women that a mode of living which doesn't push her around will reflect itself in her face and manner, and do more for her appearance than make-up and hairdo?

By the time you have those two questions solved it will be time to get up and get breakfast, then wash and iron the living room curtains.

5

All those pesky so-and-so's

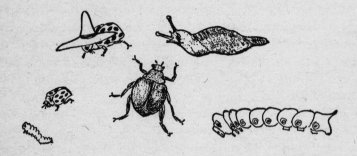

From time to time we run across some new item someone has thought up to distinguish man from mere animals, and here is my contribution; animals kill other living creatures at their convenience, unhampered by any ideas about loving kindness or brotherhood, because they have no such thoughts. Men do have these lofty ideals but they also are unhampered by them.

We aren't concerned here with man's tremendous goings-on in killing each other, killing animals to eat, or to wear, or killing just for the sport of it; the kind of murder I'm going to discuss, Gentlemen of the Jury, is considered allowable because it's a matter of self-defense. We grow food in order to eat it and thus sustain life and health, not only for ourselves but also for our helpless children, so we have a right to protect it, haven't we? Besides, all we have to do to see that killing is a Law of Nature is to glance around us.

Are you perhaps confused by now, wondering which side I'm on? Well, I vary. I can write a child's verse:

> *Pitter patter, pitter patter,*
> *Little mice make ladies scatter,*
> *But they're harmless as you please,*
> *Only want a bite of cheese.*

But when they begin to play havoc in the pantry, what can one do but get out the mouse trap? Self-protection.

That creature called man is busy today, not to say hectic, trying to defend himself from big and little enemies. He makes an impressive showing with his bombs which can wipe out quite a sizable number of his fellow beings with one blast, but he looks a bit puny when he undertakes to eliminate something the size of a mosquito or aphis and keep it eliminated without getting into hot water, not to say boiling.

Shall we begin with that inexcusable little so-and-so, the Mexican Bean Beetle? In my first book I said I hadn't seen a single one of these creatures since I had begun to mulch, which was true; automatically they had disappeared. Then what happened? The book came out, a few hundred people visited my garden and so did, that same summer, several million Mexican Bean Beetles just for the purpose, it seemed, of making a liar out of me. And they have shown up one season since then, but that's only twice in eighteen years of mulching.

I have never been troubled with the corn borer, and only one season in thirty years of gardening (by both the old and new methods) have I seen enough corn ear-worms to cause me any concern; this one visitation happened during the second advent of the bean beetles. There was a worm in every ear, I think, and that summer the local grocer told me that he had given up selling corn because all of it was so infested with worms.

You have no doubt been told that diseased plants, and any that are infected with bugs, should be taken off somewhere and burnt. In any case, they certainly mustn't be left in the garden. Which sounds reasonable even to me, an A-Number-One doubter, yet that fall I didn't get around to removing those infected stalks and vines, and in spite of my disobedience of the rules, not a beetle nor an ear-worm have I seen since. That was about six years ago.

Aren't we also told to spray tomato plants the minute

they are set out? Well, I haven't sprayed mine for eighteen years and am not troubled with either blight or bugs; other mulchers have had the same experience.

I have little that is new to report about moles. My good luck continues: no mole trouble since I began to mulch. I have had at least a hundred letters, I think, exclusively about moles, half of the writers reproaching me because my system attracts this little pest, the other half blessing me because the mulch has driven the moles away. You can draw your own conclusion, as I have done.

One man said that in an unmulched garden he can see the runs and do something before the plants are ruined, but that under hay the run is hidden. I suppose that's true; as I look back I remember that it was a sickly plant which used to call my attention to the run, which certainly wouldn't be as satisfactory as noticing it before the plant showed ill effects.

Through the past six years of letters, visitors, and talks at garden clubs, I must have heard dozens of suggestions of how to deal with moles. And my objection to all of them, except a trap, is that you never know whether or not you had anything to do with the fact that they disappeared for a season or two. They may just have decided, of their own free will, to visit a neighbor, or to transfer their activities from the asparagus bed to the corn belt.

One visitor told me something that you might like to try: he finds the entrance hole (and for me, that's the catch; how does he do that?) and puts a mouse trap near it, baited with bread. I think he said he caught seventeen moles in four weeks that way.

I am rather thoroughly convinced that proper mulching outwits cutworms. For years I felt secure, then I had a plant or two taken, and in each case I found that the hay wasn't drawn up closely to the plant. Apparently this is necessary. Last year seemed to be a cutworm season; everyone was having trouble with them, so I took special care to see that everything was closely mulched, and didn't lose a single plant.

Running through the chapter called *Enemy Aliens,* in my first book, I see that I mentioned neither the squash borer nor the cabbage worm, probably because I didn't know what to say; since then I have read a couple of heartening things which are still in the theoretical stage but well worth trying.

I came across two different articles about the squash borer, tried both suggestions, and both have worked for me, so far. First, I read that if you will help the vine of your squash take root here and there as it grows, that even if the borer kills off the vine in the hill where you put the seed, the rest of the plant will live and bear fruit. All you need do is pull the mulch from under the vine in a few places and put a little dirt on it. I tried this for a year or two and it worked.

Then I read that you can defeat the borer by putting a handful or two of cigarette ashes in the hill when you plant the seeds. Since a nicotine spray is recommended for taking care of this pest, the suggestion sounded feasible and I tried it. However, being a coward and also extra fond of Blue Hubbard squash (the only one, in my experience, that the borer goes for), I also rooted the vine and therefore proved nothing as far as tobacco goes.

But the last two years I felt either brave or lazy (take your choice) and only used the ashes in the hill, skipping the vine rooting, and got fine squash and not a borer. As I said, this is still in the theoretical stage but I'm beginning to be convinced.

It's a hard pill for us Americans to have to swallow, we who are the Biggest and the Richest and the Smartest and the Best, and I would hate to have anyone choke on it, but it's true that we sometimes "discover" some great truth or "new" trick which some "inferior" country has practiced for generations. Surprisingly often, when I've reported some idea or other that we Brilliant Americans have just thought up to a visitor who was born and raised in some far-off land, he has replied: "Oh yes, we have always done it that way." And he even says it with a sort of casual modesty.

I am leading up to the cabbage worm. A few years ago I read that the solution to that headache was salt, and the idea came from a *real* American—an Indian. If you sprinkle a little salt (not too much) on young cabbage plants and the other members of this family, you are supposed to have no cabbage worms, or, I believe, any other pests or diseases on these plants. I have often seen the leaves of cauliflower and broccoli looking most unattractive from, presumably, the presence of some insect or disease, but I've always been hazy as to what was going on.

I wrote to the author of the article containing the salt information, and received a long letter in reply; he said the same treatment could be used on turnips, and, I believe, radishes.

Deciding to try the salt, but fearful of putting on too much, I used the table shaker, sprinkling it on lightly. I've done this for the past three years and haven't seen one cabbage worm in that time. What pleases me even more is that it seemed to save the turnips. I didn't know why they had been behaving so badly in recent years—thrips, I suppose. Anyway, either they suddenly turned over a new leaf of their own accord, or the salt has done the trick.

I once said to a college professor of agriculture that it seemed unnecessary to spray cabbage with poison to get rid of worms, for if you took off the outer leaves you still had a good head; he replied that grocers won't handle cabbage which has had the outer leaves removed, and that people won't buy unsanitary heads full of worm holes. Worm holes are unsanitary, poison is sanitary. An interesting conception.

Now to our visitors who were brought up in Europe; I think these particular ones were from Lithuania. I told them about the salt for worms, thrips, and so on, and one of the women said:

"Oh yes, my father always did that but he first dissolved

the salt in water—"

She didn't even insult my intelligence by explaining why her father dissolved it and I won't insult yours. I shall certainly do it that way from now on. A mild solution.

Some people believe that mulch attracts slugs, sowbugs, mice, rats, snakes, actually sometimes giving me the impression that they think I invented these animals just to make it hard for gardeners. I have never seen any of these pests in our garden with the exception of a few dozen slugs on lettuce or cabbage through the years. There are rats, mice, and snakes here and there around the place, but the mulched spots obviously have no special attraction for them.

Through my early years of gardening and up to perhaps seven or eight years ago, I heard and read nothing about slugs. Then suddenly one needed only to glance through the farm journals to see what a prominent place they had come to occupy as a garden enemy. And since the idea of my method began to spread only a little later, it's understandable that people who have adopted it and who also are pestered with slugs might blame the mulch.

Too, slugs like a wet spot and mulch keeps the ground moist, so gardeners use that combination to convince themselves that the two go together. Like many of us who want to prove something, they ignore certain facts; in this case, that slugs also abound in unmulched plots. Of course they can still insist that mulch makes them worse, if they feel that way.

Dick Clemence has this to say: "Parts of my garden do not get the full sun all day, and slugs are a minor nuisance in these places. This is true, however, whether or not there happens to be mulch in these places. If anything, the hay helps to discourage slugs by drying out so quickly on top after a wetting. Mice have never troubled me at all, and I think mulch has little to do with the question. If an area is infested with mice, they will be troublesome, anyway. I should think that a cat or two would be the answer."

I read somewhere that a shallow pan of beer put into a

garden at night will do away with slugs. (Whether they are dead or just dead-drunk in the morning, I don't know.) I wrote this to one inquirer and he answered:

"I'm certainly not going to carry beer out to the garden for slugs. If they want beer they can come in the house and ask for it, like everybody else."

J. I. Rodale's useful *Encyclopedia of Organic Gardening* (Emmaus, Pa.) has some interesting comments on slugs and snails which are worth quoting:

"Each snail and slug builds its own highway by secreting a slimy material which hardens into a silvery trail. This material not only smooths the way for these creatures, but it forces them to stick to the trail whether it be right side up or upside down. Slugs can even form mucous ropes for suspending themselves from supports or for going from one level to another. When snails decide to move it takes them about 15 days to travel one mile, while slugs can cover the same distance in about eight days. Slugs differ from snails by having no shell or a mere rudiment of a shell.

"These animals cannot stand dry conditions. During periods of drought, snails place a pane of "glass" over the entrance to their shell house. A film of mucous is stretched across the entrance to the shell. This quickly hardens into a transparent "window pane." In the same way, they close their house for the winter. But in winter the door is barred with a heavy pane that is not transparent.

F. C. King of Cumberland, England, an unusually observant gardener and writer, suggests that the lack of earthworms and consequently of worm casts on the land today is giving rise to the terrible slug menace. Worm casts are alkaline and thus inimical to slugs which seek a more acid soil for their abode. Mulch makes earthworms, so it should eventually chase away slugs.

"CONTROL: Snails and slugs tend to be nocturnal, i.e. they move about and feed at night but rest in a dark, cool, moist place by day. Advantage may be taken of this habit to eliminate them from your garden if they are troublesome.

Place shingles or other similar materials in the garden to serve as traps. Each morning destroy the individuals which have hidden away under the traps for the day.

"The body of snails and slugs is soft and highly sensitive to such sharp objects as sand and slag and to such dry and slightly corrosive substances as slaked lime and wood ashes. A narrow border of sharp sand or cinders around a bed or border will serve as an effective barrier against them. A sprinkling of slaked lime or wood ashes along a row of tender plants will keep the snails and slugs away because their soft bodies are sensitive to these materials."

For the past three years some creatures have been eating our tomatoes as they began to ripen. I have no slugs, so that isn't it. One visitor told me it was mourning doves; he had caught them at it. I doubt that this is so in my patch, for the bite is often under the fruit. Once I found a cricket in a half-eaten job, but had he been feasting or was he merely resting in a cool spot on a hot day? Mice? Chipmunks? I never caught either of those doing it, or even in the garden at all.

You can do one of two things about this: stake the tomatoes, or (as I do) every few days tuck some newspaper around the biggest and best-looking ones which are beginning to turn color. And you can also gather them before they are fully ripe.

I have nothing to add to what I have said previously about Japanese beetles which was that we have none, and I've not a word to say about the spraying of all the fruit we eat (not to mention the by-product of poisoning the men who do the job). And I will also skip the fantastic antics of men who do a comprehensive job of indiscriminate murder from airplanes. These problems are for better minds than mine, and these big brains had better get busy before they deteriorate along with their over-fed, undernourished bodies; then we shall be lost indeed.

But I am still using such brains as I have in the battle against woodchucks and rabbits. I have written about these creatures off and on, and at length, but I'm sorry to say that I was talking primarily about all the things that don't work rather than any that do.

Although I am very cautious about recommending anything until I have tried it, I went so far a year ago as to say to audiences and in print that I was sure you could keep these pests out of a garden if you planted a fence of soybeans all around it. I had heard this some years before but hadn't tried it because I was then using some long wire cages which I put over the more tempting crops; these were effective but they finally wore out. I didn't replace them, then later somebody again mentioned the soybean treatment.

I not only decided to try it but wrote about it in advance; I felt sure it would work because through all the years, if there were any soybeans in the garden, both woodchucks and rabbits went straight for them, and unless I protected them somehow, they were cleaned out before anything else was touched. And in order to get to the beans they often had to pass close to tender beets and kohlrabi, two of their preferred vegetables. So wasn't it obvious that with a mass of soybeans growing all around your garden everything else would be safe?

Well, there are two things wrong with that reasoning. One is that soybeans can't be planted until danger of frost is past, by which time early crops such as lettuce, beets, kohlrabi are up and thriving and offering a tempting meal to animals. Let us say, though, that we can protect these few early things; I did, and planted the soybeans a little later with optimism.

The other drawback is that woodchucks don't wait for a vegetable to mature; when the beans were an inch high the animals began on them, and you can imagine how long it took one woodchuck to clean up a couple of hundred feet of soy beans of that height.

In other words, the idea doesn't work.

The man who cut our hay last summer said he had never

seen so many rabbits in one field, and dozens of people have told me that that was the worst season for woodchucks they had ever known. I too had never suffered so much from them as I did last year, and as I clumsily tried to protect one thing after another, I discovered that if pushed to the wall they will settle for things which I would have said were safe, such as carrot tops and parsley.

There's no point in going into detail about the damage they did, but I do want to tell about the cabbage family. That was difficult to protect, so I tried only halfheartedly, then gave up. All leaves were eaten, leaving only stalks. I didn't give them a final thinning, hoping that if I left plenty, the marauders might skip one·here or there. Just an optimist.

My neighbor offered me some of her cabbage plants, and I said: "For the woodchucks to enjoy?"

"But you must have a garden!" she exclaimed.

"Who says I must? Lots of people manage without one."

She knew that it was a desperate woman speaking, not a philosopher, and she went to Pierre, her husband, with the gloomy tale. Being as sympathetic as she, he came over at once with a proposition: if we wanted to buy the material, he would shop for it and put up a fence around our garden.

There is also no use going into the reasons why we had never tried a fence, but the main one was that gardeners who had them were forever reporting that animals got into their plot either over or under the fence. However, the way I felt now, it was any port in a storm and a drowning man grabs at a straw and any other appropriate cliché you can think up.

The fence turned out to be inadequate, which was nobody's fault, just a combination of circumstances. I believe that a fence will keep animals out, provided it is put into the ground deeply enough (ours is only a few inches deep), and if it flares out at the top, so that when an animal climbs it he will find himself under a sort of wire roof. Fred thought this up (perhaps others have, too), and I don't believe the theory has a single weak spot, as the idea of the soybean fence has.

For a week or so our fence did seem to have the animals thwarted, then one morning I discovered that the soybeans I had planted inside the garden were being eaten. I didn't find a hole under the fence so assumed the pest had climbed over. I got to work and fixed up the fanciest contraption you ever saw with a long piece of chicken wire.

Now back to the cabbage family: that same morning I saw to my surprise that they were all putting out new leaves, and through the war that followed, now the woodchuck winning, now me, those plants went backward and forward, over and over, sometimes all eaten off again, then again making new leaves. Three of the early cabbages actually made decent heads, one purple cauliflower and two white ones produced small ones, and by middle October all of the plants were large, green, and healthy-looking, although nothing else had time to mature.

I tell about this because I was so impressed by it. I have never been able to figure out why the "will to live" is spoken of as though it was something to be admired. If you are hopelessly ill why is it in your favor to put up a fight against death? If you are miserably unhappy, what's against wishing you could die? For that matter, if you are religious and even if you are reasonably happy, what's bad about being in a hurry to get to heaven? Yet I marveled at (and, I suppose, admired) those plants which came back, and back again, in the tremendous effort to fulfill their destiny.

Back to our inadequate fence. Apparently raccoons (or maybe squirrels) crawled over it to get to the corn, but I've already told you how I protect that crop. Before long I found evidence that a woodchuck had crawled under the fence and I blocked up the hole. And he went under at another spot, which I had expected him to do.

So instead of blocking this second hole, I bent a ten-foot piece of heavy, wide, hardware cloth in the middle length-

. . . The fence turned out to be inadequate, which was nobody's fault, just a combination of circumstances. . . . . For a week or so it did seem to have the animals thwarted, then one morning I discovered that the soybeans I had planted inside the garden were being eaten.

wise and placed it so that the woodchuck would enter it when he came through that hole again. I stuffed the open end so that he couldn't go on through, but in such a way that I could tell if he tried to. And in case he got the bright idea of digging under this long cage, I put old feed-sacks under it, to baffle him.

The next morning there was the evidence; he had tried to get through and had failed, and the question is: why didn't he, when he went out again, dig under the fence somewhere else? I don't know what *your* answer to that is, but here's mine: my scheme did what I had hoped it would— made a neurotic of him, or a coward, or both. He no doubt thought to himself: if this is what happens, now, when I come through a hole, goodness knows what else I might be up against if I should try another spot.

This was in August, and he didn't come back, but of course I couldn't rely on that sort of thing. And since we didn't want to go to the expense of putting up another—a "proper"—fence, I began making all sorts of plans.

Someone told me that a piece of chicken wire, placed flat on the ground along a fence, would nonplus woodchucks; they can't dig *right by* the fence and apparently can't figure out that they could go back a few feet and start there. This sounded reasonable to me, but for the time being I decided to rely on the strips of paper and cardboard which I had (through the winter) put all around the garden outside the fence. My purpose in doing this is to kill the witchgrass but I believe it will also confuse the woodchucks.

However, there was still the question of what to do if they climbed over the fence, and one morning about the middle of June (this was when the fence had been up about a year) there was every indication that some animal had done just that; it had had about a five-course meal, and it hadn't got in *under* the fence.

There were two woodchuck holes near the south end of the garden plot, so I took a 40-foot length of chicken wire (all I had) and fastened it to the top of the fence along that end with very heavy string, so that it made a sort of floppy roof along the top of the fence. And I strengthened it here and there with wire coat hangers, bent into a long, partly double piece. This was all done more than a little on the optimistic side (not to say stupid) since all the animals had to do was go a little further down the fence where the obstruction stopped.

And they did shortly get in again. I desperately covered the vegetables they preferred, then decided to protect even their second-best choice, and I finally also covered the plants that they would settle for in a pinch. And I went out to the garden over and over at various hours of the day in an effort to catch one inside. At last I was lucky and saw a woodchuck making an escape over the fence when I approached.

So they were climbing the fence, and I needed only that evidence for proof for Fred and John. (Usually a man looks at you as if he were sure you had left the gate open if you tell him an animal got in the garden.) I was relieved, because I felt I had to have masculine brains to help me decide what to do—that is, the most effective and least expensive way of fastening a wire roof on top of the fence, one which the beasts couldn't handle.

One conference followed another, and in the meantime the woodchuck went on to the parsnips and a few other things he had so far ignored. Finally I diffidently (and somewhat embarrassedly) said to John: "Come out and I'll show you what I fixed up at that one end."

Well, he examined the wobbly wire contraption, then suddenly snapped his fingers and exclaimed: "That's it! It's so weak and shaky that they couldn't possibly scale it." We had bought some more chicken wire and John fastened it all along the top of the whole fence with pieces of heavy string and strands of wire. And since then the animals have been settling for what they find elsewhere.

I have saved to the last those little creatures beloved by all which rob us of berries and cherries—the birds. Perhaps you have a feeder for them where they can gorge, and even though you can't really afford it, you may build a bird-bath for their pleasure, but don't look for any consideration in return; after all, they have never heard about gratitude.

We have no cherry trees, and if we had I have no idea what one might do to protect the fruit. Not many of our raspberries are taken, but some man from Pennsylvania told us that birds took almost his entire crop; he has built some sort of tent which lets the bees in and keeps the birds out. He said he would send me a description of the contraption, but I'm afraid he has forgotten his promise.

In my first garden book I described at length how we protect strawberries from frost and birds, which is a rather elaborate and expensive process involving movable cold frames ten feet long and extra screens made of heavy wire netting. Recently I met a man, who lives in Florida, who makes a contraption which answers this and other purposes; I will describe it in chapter VII where we face the frost problem.

Some people answer this bird question by suggesting that everyone grow enough for them too. Well, that's fine, but just don't let that business of "eating like a bird" fool

. . . People often answer this question by suggesting that everyone grow enough for the birds too. That's fine, but just don't let that business of "eating like a bird" fool you; they seem to dine almost every waking moment, and I've heard tales about their consuming, every day, what amounts to five times their weight. . . . .

you; they seem to gorge almost every waking moment, and I've heard tales about their consuming, every day, what amounts to five times their weight. So better take a paper and pencil and figure out how much one hundred birds weigh, multiply by five, and see how many pounds (or quarts) of berries that amounts to. And unless you are in the business of selling them, and have an acre or so, I have a feeling that you will somehow come out much as I did when I tried to plant enough soybeans for the woodchucks.

The defense rests.

6

Where to plant what

It is October, and I trust your garden looks terrible, with dead vines, corn stalks, clumsy cabbage roots—refuse—all over it. And I do hope you will leave everything there, and add the kitchen garbage to it through the winter.

I used to put the coarser things, such as corn stalks and roots of cabbage, between the rows of asparagus, where they wouldn't be a nuisance the following spring, but this is unnecessary work; the stalks are pretty well rotted by the following May, and the corn roots, which I leave in the ground, are either entirely rotted or enough so that I can easily pull them out if they are in the way of planting.

And now that I've decided that rotating crops is nonsense, I put the cabbage family where it was before. Also, since I plant everything which should be spaced a foot or more apart by dropping a few seeds in the spots where I want the one final plant to be (see zinnias in Chapter IX) the refuse around doesn't get in the way.

For many years I rotated my crops, not because the scientists had me buffaloed in this respect, but because it seemed as easy to do as not, so why not humor them? Then I decided that it actually wasn't quite as easy, so I began the revolt by asking myself if it was necessary in my way of gardening where the soil was constantly renewed by rotting mulch. The next question was: why don't we also have to rotate asparagus, rhubarb, raspberries, roses, and oak trees? Our asparagus has been producing on the same spot for thirty years. My final step was to stop rotating and nothing seems to object so far. By the way, ever since my rhubarb has been fed with nothing but kitchen garbage (eighteen years) it makes excellent eating right through October. Experts tell you not to cut it longer than eight or ten weeks.

Through October and November there are a number of jobs to do which are related to the garden but only two which I *must* do if I want to feel I have done my duty. One is to cover the strawberries properly; after a few light frosts I put on a thin layer of hay, and when around 20 degree weather seems imminent, I pile it on good and thick. The other job, which I didn't mention in my first book because I didn't know it then, seems to be helpful: in the middle of winter, when the cold weather is here to stay, I broadcast cotton seed meal over both flower and vegetable gardens at the rate of five pounds to every one hundred square feet. Any other meal would answer the same purpose, I'm told, except corn meal for corn.

Fred made two ten-foot lengths of wood for me to use as measuring sticks; I place these at right angles to each other, scatter five pounds of meal, then move the sticks to the next section. However, it's safe to abandon both measuring the space and weighing the meal after you have done this a few times for you will know just about how much you need.

Some time ago I read a rather convincing article which said that rotting vegetable matter supplied everything a soil needed except nitrogen. I sent the article to Scott Nearing, one of my foremost advisers and asked him: if this were true, what should I do? He told me to add cotton seed or soy bean meal but he didn't say how much.

So I most haphazardly scattered meal around. Finally, Dr. Pratt, of Cornell, gave me the above proportions, and also said that if you add the meal in the winter you can put it on top of the mulch, that rain and snow will wash it through to the soil. And the obliging thing about cotton seed meal seems to be that it doesn't release the nitrogen until warm weather and that, of course, is when the soil wants it. So much for the past, but Dick tells me that he thinks I could probably get along now without adding any nitrogen; next season I'll do a little experimenting along these lines.

As fall approaches I find my passion for playing around

with soil cooling considerably, and have to coax myself into putting in late spinach and lettuce. And even dill, without which none of our meals except breakfast is complete. (Come to think of it, what's wrong with a bit of fresh dill on breakfast toast?)

The leaves are all raked up now, and disposed of, and by that I of course don't mean burned. When like a leaf I wither, fall, and die, and St. Peter asks me what I've done to deserve to enter Paradise I will say:

"Well, off hand, I can't think of a single thing. But I'll tell you something I *haven't* done: I've never burned a pile of leaves." This may not get me a preferred seat but I bet a bale of hay it will see me through the gate.

Here's a suggestion for you who prefer shredded leaves: instead of buying a machine, carting the leaves to it, shredding them, then taking them to the garden, why don't you rake them up and dump them in your driveway? After a few cars have gone over them they will be expertly shredded. Remove them and dump another batch in the path of the cars.

At last all the leaves and some woodchips are spread over flower and vegetable plots, the ground freezes, snow falls, and I'm not sorry there isn't a thing I can do for the garden for awhile except, perhaps, cut a few bean poles with a miniature axe; a vacation from anything, no matter how much one may enjoy it, is welcome. I do have to continue to write a garden column each week but that's the only attention I will have to give this activity until spring.

Oh that's nonsense, I had forgotten about the seed catalogs which show up immediately after Christmas, and everyone knows what these do to a gardener; it's like offering catnip to a cat.

I learned long ago that you can hardly do anything more wasteful of time than to start to plant without a complete, detailed plan on paper. So, when the catalogs arrive and, surprisingly, the fever to get going begins to flicker, I get a measuring stick and go out and measure my plot.

Now, I would be embarrassed if anyone asked me how it is that I don't know the size of my garden. I do cut it down slightly once in awhile, but I can't use this for an excuse, now that it is fenced. However, I can still say (although it really doesn't make much sense) that my plot isn't cut and dried, that perennials, such as rhubarb and raspberries, aren't spaced as regularly as might be desired.

It may be that for some strange reason I actually enjoy going out there on a cold day and fumbling around in bare hands with paper and pencil and measuring sticks, though I admit it's difficult to grasp since I don't like to feel shivery. So if I insist on doing this measuring each year, I wonder why I don't do it in pleasant weather, since I'm not a confirmed procrastinator in other fields of activity.

But my next job is indeed a cozy one. With a large heavy sheet of white paper, a pencil with an eraser, a small ruler, my favorite seed catalog, and preferably with glowing logs in the fireplace, I get comfortable on the couch and make a diagram of next year's planting.

And now another question arises, this one easier to answer: since I don't rotate crops, why make such a project of this? Don't I plant more or less the same things in the same quantity year after year? Well, no, not entirely. For instance, last year I planted a rather long row of celeriac which I hadn't done for years. And twice as much celery as the season before, and more of the cabbage family. I always make a few changes.

Even after thirty years of experience, I seem to come up with some small improvement every time I make a new plan. And I've always had the vain hope that somehow I would be able to choose a good spot for the edible pod peas which grow tall but also droopy, and demand more space than seems justified. Now that my garden is fenced, this problem is solved: I of course plant them along the fence. And stubbornly I go over and over the problem of wandering pumpkin and squash vines (especially Blue Hubbard) which seem to have less restraint than anything, unless it's

Japanese honeysuckle and Russian sunflowers.

If saving either money or time is important to you, of course the smaller your garden the better. Although my method cuts down the labor unbelievably, it does take time to spread mulch, and there's surely no point in covering

— GARDEN ON PAPER FIRST —

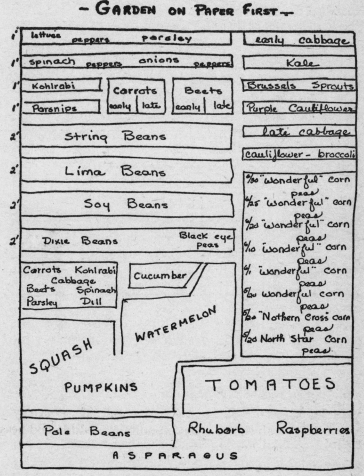

1' lettuce peppers parsley	early cabbage
1' spinach peppers onions peppers	Kale
1' Kohlrabi / Carrots early late / Beets early late	Brussels Sprouts
1' Parsnips	Purple Cauliflower
2' String Beans	late cabbage
2' Lima Beans	cauliflower - broccoli
2' Soy Beans	⁹/₃₀ "wonderful" corn peas

String Beans, Lima Beans, Soy Beans, Dixie Beans / Black eye peas

Carrots Kohlrabi Cabbage
Beets Spinach
Parsley Dill

Cucumber

⁹/₃₀ "wonderful" corn / peas
⁴/₂₅ "wonderful" corn / peas
⁴/₂₀ "wonderful" corn / peas
⁴/₁₀ "wonderful" corn / peas
⁴/₁ "wonderful" corn / peas
⁵/₂₀ wonderful corn / peas
⁵/₂₀ "Nothern Cross corn / peas
⁵/₂₀ North Star Corn / peas

SQUASH WATERMELON

PUMPKINS   TOMATOES

Pole Beans   Rhubarb   Raspberries

ASPARAGUS

. . . But my next job is a cozy one indeed. With a large sheet of heavy white paper, a pencil with an eraser, a small ruler, my favorite seed catalog, and preferably with glowing logs in the fireplace, I get comfortable on the couch and make a diagram of next year's planting.

more ground than one needs. Or in spending more money for cotton seed meal and mulch than is necessary.

In the saving of space, planning next season's garden in the winter, when one can take time to give it some thought and isn't pushed by a dozen other jobs, as is likely to be the case in spring, is invaluable. I sit and cogitate, gaze into the fire, then close my eyes and use some imagination. Most important, I can change my mind; if, for instance, a row of parsnips has been placed on the diagram in an inconvenient spot, I need nothing but the eraser to move it, but if it's already planted before I discover the error, then it must either stay where it is, or another row will have to be put in somewhere else, or I will have to skip parsnips that season.

Here are a few space-saving suggestions which may have eluded you. (For the rest of your plan you don't need any help from me.) I will list the vegetables alphabetically for your convenience, and, also, to make sure I don't overlook something.

BEANS: I believe pole limas are the most satisfactory for most people and take up least space; I can't grow them on account of our short season. Bush limas may be planted (two or three seeds every eight inches) in the early lettuce row, for they won't be needing much room until after the lettuce is harvested.

A row of bush green beans will give you an earlier crop than the pole variety so I plant a few of them. Here, if you like, you can leave a space every foot or so and put in some branch of the cabbage family. Almost anything may be planted near or between the bean poles.

BEETS can be planted twelve inches from any crop which won't grow large enough to overshadow them, such as parsnips or celery.

CABBAGE FAMILY: early and late cabbage, broccoli, cauliflower, kale, Brussels sprouts. Now that my soil is so rich from rotting mulch, I plant a few seeds twelve inches apart in the row, thinning them to one plant, and space the rows twelve inches apart; this, even though they have a reputation for being gross feeders.

CARROTS: Chapter VIII consists of things I have learned from others, but have tried only once or perhaps not at all. Here you will find a novel way of planting carrots.

CAULIFLOWER: (See cabbage family).

CELERY: Twelve inches from anything.

CHINESE CABBAGE: You don't need to include this in your planting plan; it is supposed to be put in quite late, and I'm sure you'll find some spot for it when the time comes.

COLLARDS: If you are crowded for space you can wait until summer to plant this, then put it in some spot which has finished with some early crop. This way you will have these greens after several frosts.

CORN: Rows two feet apart, plants eight inches apart in the row.

CUCUMBERS: (see Vine crops).

DILL: I don't include this in my plan, but I plant it all summer long and about every two or three weeks, in some small spot that isn't occupied, sowing three or four feet of it each time.

EGG PLANT: We don't like it when *I* cook it, so I don't grow it.

HERBS: Not in my plan. If you grow them to any appreciable extent you will probably have a separate herb garden.

HORSE RADISH: I would rather do almost anything than grate it so I don't grow it.

KALE: (see cabbage family).

KOHLRABI: Plant twelve inches from anything which won't grow large enough to shade it or droop over it.

LEEKS: Onions suit us well enough, so I don't bother with these.

LETTUCE: I reserve a space in the diagram for only the first planting; after that, I always seem to be able to find an empty spot for it. What's wrong with putting it, especially summer plantings, between the asparagus or the corn rows, since it likes shade in hot weather? Some people go through all sorts of performances (nets, and so on) to shade their lettuce, when there's often adequate protection from the sun all around, going begging.

If you prefer to wait until lettuce has headed before picking it, your first meal of it will be quite a while coming; also, you will require considerable space if you follow the rules and plant it eighteen inches apart. But if you like leaf lettuce, you can get surprisingly many salads from a twenty-foot row.

Plant your favorite variety of head lettuce, and don't thin it until it's large enough to eat; that is, two or three inches high. Thinning it and washing what you pull out for the table is somewhat tedious, and you probably wouldn't bother with it later on in the season when you've already been eating freshly-picked things. But at that early stage you may be willing to go to this trouble, and the plants grow very fast; almost before you know it the job lightens, and the only problem is to pick it often enough, so that the plants which you are going to let head will have a chance to do so. With my very good soil (and made that way, don't forget, from rotting mulch) I get fine large heads from plants that have been crowded until they are fairly big, and which at best aren't more than eight to twelve inches apart.

MUSKMELON: (see Vine crops).

OKRA: We don't care for it.

ONIONS: If you are short on space, leave them out of the diagram; you can toss sets on some hay just anywhere, outside your plot. However, for large sweet Spanish onions, the plants need some garden space.

PARSLEY: Plant twelve inches from anything that won't shade it.

PARSNIPS: The tops get rather big but they stand up straight; it's safe to plant as close to them as 12 inches. On the other hand they can hold their own in competition with things such as lima beans.

PEAS: Between the corn rows for the regular kind. I grow Edible Pods along the fence. Joseph Harris doesn't carry these; I get them from W. Atlee Burpee Co. (Hunting Park Ave. at 18th St., Philadelphia, Pa.) or from Burgess.

PEPPERS: I buy plants and put them in the row of spinach, which has been picked by the time the peppers need more room.

POTATOES: You can lay these on the ground, outside the garden if you wish, and put hay on them.

PUMPKINS: (see Vine crops).

RADISHES: Need no space of their own; the seeds can be dropped in the carrot, parsley, parsnip rows.

RUTABAGA: Space six inches apart.

SPINACH: Since it matures so early it may be planted twelve inches from anything at all. However, if you're going to (as I do) put peppers in the same row, you mustn't plant the spinach too close to big floppy things such as edible soy beans.

SQUASH: (see Vine crops). Zuccini squash, which doesn't make vines, may be planted among the corn.

SWISS CHARD: Fred and my sister don't like it so I don't grow it.

TOMATOES: If you stake them they need less space than if you let them roam. Mine wander, so I put them between the corn and raspberries or along the fence.

TURNIPS: No need to put these in the diagram, unless you plant rutabaga, in which case you might want to reserve a place for them. I plant white turnips at the end of July and have always been able to find a good-sized spot for them, where something else is either finished or just about to call it a day.

VINE CROPS: These are a prize headache. I have already told you what I plan to do next season to quell the ardor of Blue Hubbard squash, but that solves only a very small part of the problem. Theoretically, putting them at the edge of the garden, so that they will do their traveling out on the field, sounds good, but they don't go exactly where you intend them to; they either can't read your mind or don't give a hang about what *you* want.

For years I put them in the corn patch and they did all right. For that matter they themselves always do fine; it's you and the nearby vegetables which suffer. When they are among the corn it's next to impossible not to trample the vines, so I finally abandoned that practice. So far I haven't been able to think up anything better than putting them along the asparagus row, and also at the end of the garden, and I'll control them the best I can. If we didn't like them all so much, I suppose I would be relieved if some reliable authority (where is he?) would come out with the information that squash, pumpkin, cucumbers, and melons have no nutritive value.

WATERMELON: see Vine crops—and do try *Sugar Baby!*

Now, in your eagerness to make a diagram, don't do it before you read chapter VIII. Dick Clemence has just come up with some radical suggestions which I will briefly tell you about there.

When my plan is complete, I order the seeds, and I don't quite understand those people (and I believe there are a great many) who don't get this ordering job off their hands in winter. I am particularly baffled by those who wait to buy their seeds until they are ready to plant them, then have to get them at a store instead of from a seed-house.

What's wrong with that? Well, for one thing, if you know what varieties you prefer, can you always get them at that late hour? For another, can you be sure that the seeds you buy over a counter aren't left-overs from another year? Business is business, we are told, which seems to imply that men in business are as a rule trustworthy only insofar as it increases their bank balance.

You may now be thinking that this also applies to a seed-house; it is a business firm. True, but if the people at the head of it are intelligent, they realize that it's to their advantage to be careful not to sell worthless seeds. But how much does a storekeeper lose if he sells a package of seeds which don't germinate? They are only one small item in his business.

I am reminded of a time some years ago when I wanted a certain variety of melon which Joseph Harris had always listed but which was missing that year in their catalog. I wrote and asked them about it and Mr. Warren sent me a large package of the seeds but wouldn't let me pay for them because they were a year old; this firm has a reputation for handling satisfactory seeds, and they intend to keep that standing by deserving it. Incidentally those seeds did germinate.

If you happen to be a last-minute seed buyer I doubt if I've said anything to change you, for I believe such things are a matter of temperament rather than of thought. Perhaps it is, though, to some small extent, a thought-out thing; you may feel that you might forget some item if you order so far in advance, or that you may change your mind about something.

Well, if you find that you failed to order some seeds that you want, it will cost you only a few minutes of time and a stamp to take care of that. And even if you order a couple of things which you decide you don't want to plant, you will have wasted very little money, and will probably know of someone who can use the seeds.

Let's say that you do send your order in January, and in due time the seeds arrive. You surely look them over, to see that they are all there, and maybe you arrange them alphabetically or according to when you are going to plant them. I put mine into three boxes, marked Early, Middle, Late, then arrange the envelopes alphabetically.

February shows up. But wasn't it only yesterday that I said "Pleasant dreams" to my garden, feeling that I had a long stretch of time when I could turn my enthusiasm to something else? Yet almost any day now Fred will announce: "I don't care what the calendar says, this is a spring day."

A crocus opens its eyes. A redwing calls. You love winter, you really do, but this is something quite different. You hear the garden summoning you, and you call back: "Yes, yes, coming!"

7

Jack Frost and a children's garden

In my thirty years of gardening, July is the only month in which we haven't had at least one frost. Some years ago we had one in August and we've had quite a number in June, and even though I have at last worked out a relatively easy way to keep plants from freezing, I'm sure the cold retards them. Yet it would make too short a season if I waited until the latter part of June to put in the sensitive things which are affected by cold nights.

There are people (and some of them thoughtful, intelligent; reasoning men, and organic gardeners to boot) who, without ever having tried my system of mulching, love to pick flaws in it. One of them states in his garden book that he knows of a tomato crop that froze one night in June *because it was mulched* (italics mine) while his own unmulched plants, not ten miles away, were unharmed.

It's a depressing thing to find such a carelessly-drawn conclusion in a book which had seemed sound enough to me until I came across that statement. I am now wondering what else he has said which has no authentic basis.

How do I know that the above conclusion was reckless? Because my own garden freezes when the one directly across the road from me, not two hundred yards away, isn't affected; last season my tomatoes were taken by frost in early September, while this same neighbor's crop was harvested until late in October. And *both* gardens are heavily mulched.

I am willing to accept the *possibility* that a mulched garden is more susceptible to frost than an unmulched one, but I think it's regrettable that a man who knows enough about gardening to write a book on the subject, doesn't seem to be aware that in an area of one mile (much less ten) one garden may be killed by frost while another one is untouched, whether the two gardens are mulched or not. Here in Redding, Connecticut, everyone who grows things knows this.

My plot happens to be in a frost pocket, and through the years before I mulched, I gradually became reconciled to losing my plants while nearby gardens escaped. And sometimes I have had to escort my milkman, or a neighbor, out to the scene of disaster, for proof; they couldn't believe that we had actually had so damaging a frost.

Such a careless, incorrect conclusion as this writer draws bothers me; because if it keeps only one person from trying out my back-saving, all-over, year-round mulch method it has done harm. If only you could see the hundreds of letters I've had from old or sick or overworked people, who say they wouldn't be able to garden if they didn't do it my easy way! It makes me sad to think that anyone might be talked out of trying it, and with such faulty reasoning.

I wouldn't dream of abandoning mulching, even if I were convinced that it made my crops more susceptible to frost; the many advantages of the system would far outweigh that one disadvantage. I blundered along through many years, trying to outwit old Jack with hotkaps and other devices, but nothing really worked. Then about three seasons ago, I hit on a solution which is so simple that I was amazed it hadn't occurred to me before.

In a mulched garden there's no such thing as too much hay around. For instance, if you pile it up on both sides of rows of bush peas, the vines will stand up and be easy to pick, they won't get too wet, and they won't droop over the corn, which I have planted for years between the rows of peas. And it's a quick and simple job to put some extra hay near plants such as beans, tomatoes, peppers, and other tender crops, which in any case isn't wasted effort, because you can always distribute all of this hay around here and there, before the season is over.

Perhaps you have guessed my solution: whenever I sensed that frost was on its way (and believe me, I can always feel Jack's approach, no matter what the radio and thermometer may promise) I covered every plant except the hardiest ones with hay. And with it so handy, it's astonishing how quickly this can be done.

Even if your corn is getting rather high, you won't damage it if you gently place a gob of hay on it (that which is there beside it, propping up the peas), and the same is true of tomatoes. Also, if the following morning is cold and more frost is indicated, I've found that the covering can be left on the plants all day without ill effects.

Last season I saved my plants three different times in June. And one of those nights many of the crops (mulched and unmulched) within a radius of seven miles of us were killed by frost.

You can of course try my way whether or not you are converted to mulching. And I am hoping, in regard to non-mulchers, that when the danger of frost is past, you won't get around to moving the hay, which you will have lying about, before you just accidentally discover that there are no weeds where it is lying and that the ground under it is soft and moist and, well, why not put hay all over the plot? And leave it there for always.

The hotkaps, hot tents, and such devices manufactured and sold for frost-defeating purposes never appealed to me, although I have tried them now and then for years in a half-hearted way; finally I abandoned them. I'm not at all saying they aren't effective, I feel rather sure they are, but I find using hay quicker, simpler, cheaper.

Recently I met a man who has devised a frost-proof contraption which may appeal to you. An added advantage of it is that it may also be used to defeat birds, woodchucks, and the like. Here is his description of how to make it:

The frame is made of ¼ inch cold-rolled steel rod, spot welded. You lay down two rods, about five feet long, parallel, and nine inches apart. Spot weld, at each end and in the middle, an arched piece of rod, sixteen inches high at the center. I have been told, but do not know for sure, that such arches can be bought. In any event it is easy to bend the rod over a round log or a large pipe.

Cover this with chicken wire, ½ inch mesh. The ends are left open. When using them to keep the birds and woodchucks off your plants, set the frames close together, end to end, and place a board or screen against the two end openings.

For use against frost cut a piece of polyethylene—the .015 or .020 thickness (sometimes called 15 or 20 mil) the length of the frame and wide enough to cover it, nail to a strip of white pine at the two long edges and lay over the wire frame.

Mr. McComb says these cost about a dollar a foot to make, and I think he can be persuaded to do it for you, if you would rather not tackle it yourself, although that isn't his business. His address is Lee McComb, Box 450, Leesburg, Florida, and his real business is growing oranges, grapefruit and pineapple, which he neither sprays nor artificially colors and which he will ship to anyone who is disinclined to eat the kind one has to buy in market. The trouble is that after you have sampled his fruit, you feel as you do about your home-grown corn, asparagus, tomatoes; you are spoiled for any lesser product.

Lee has the most infectious smile and the quickest wit I've come across in a long time, and I have the feeling that the reason his fruit is so sweet is because he cheerfully kids it along and keeps it in a good humor.

As many of us know, parsnips have a better taste after they have been frozen in the ground. The catch here is that unless you're one of those heroes who will go out with a pickaxe in midwinter and dig up some, you can't have any parsnips until spring. And then you have to dig all of them up and eat them every day because they deteriorate somewhat if they are either left in the ground or kept around very long after they're dug.

Last fall I put my mind to work on this unfortunate situation, telling myself that since parsnips freeze slowly, why not dig up a big one, leave some dirt on it to make it feel that nothing unusual was going on, wrap it in quite a lot of freezer paper, put it in the warmest part of the freezer rather than the coldest (where one is told to put anything for quick freezing), leave it there for a week or two, then thaw it just as gradually as possible in the refrigerator (since parsnips thaw slowly in the ground in March), unwrap, and have a look? I did all that and what I saw was a soft worthless mass.

Undaunted, I had another bright idea: I dug up a couple of fine parsnips in late autumn, put them in a half-bushel basket filled with dirt, and put them in a shed to freeze. Then one day in midwinter I would thaw them out slowly, moving them from shed to cold pantry to kitchen, and they would surely think they were still in the ground and act accordingly.

When they were finally thawed out they were getting soft, but would probably have been rather good cooked. I was bored by now, though, with the whole thing, and threw them onto the garden plot for mulch. I don't know what went haywire, but I still think that if handled properly in this way (whatever properly might be), those parsnips should be like the ones left in the frozen earth.

I cover carrots with bales of hay in November and dig them all winter long. They should be covered, I think, after the ground has become very cold, even perhaps slightly frozen. But it doesn't freeze solid under the hay, and through the winter I need only tip over the bale, dig out whatever I want and again cover the row. Loose hay or leaves would do just as well, I suppose, but wouldn't be quite as easy to handle.

Last winter when our weather stayed very cold for a long time, and there was almost no snow, the bales froze solidly to the ground and I couldn't move them, so it didn't work out that season. However, the carrots were intact in the spring, and to us they seem crisper, fresher, sweeter, when just dug than those from either a root cellar or the freezer.

I tried this with beets only once—that same cold year, unfortunately—and they froze and turned black; I don't see why it wouldn't work in a normal year. Also, we discovered last winter that turnips are much sweeter after they have been frozen in the ground. However, I don't believe they would stick it out till spring, as parsnips do, and I haven't got the necessary enthusiasm to chop them out of the frozen earth in winter. This year I am planning to pull some dirt over both beets and turnips and put a bale of hay on them. With this treatment I believe one could dig them all winter.

The shortest season I have ever been up against was an eight-week one. This happened four years ago, when a Mrs. Doherty telephoned me in March to say that she was starting a Country Day School at her home in Ridgefield in June and would I teach the children gardening. I wanted the worst way to refuse; I was too busy, I said, I didn't drive a car, and I had no talent for handling children. But I finally gave in because I couldn't bear to think of those defenseless youngsters being taught by somebody else to garden in the old-fashioned way: spading, hoeing, cultivating, weeding, watering. Such a waste of good hours, even children's, and such a pity to start them out with bad habits!

I was to go once a week for eight successive weeks, and this short span of time meant, of course, that the seeds had to be chosen carefully, so that the children could see some results. I could think of no flowers that would grow and bloom in eight weeks. I ordered onion sets, carrots, radishes, beans, lettuce, pumpkin, cucumbers, and zuccini squash.

Mrs. Doherty drove me over to her place early in April, to show me the garden plot; it looked satisfactory, and I told her it must be covered at once with eight inches of hay and/or leaves. They had a horse so there was hay on the place.

My first session was during the last week in June; there were ten children, ranging in age from five to twelve. We

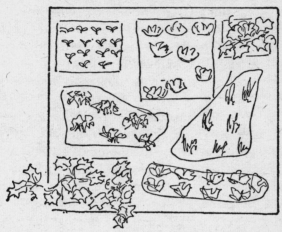

— CHILD'S 8-WEEK GARDEN —

. . . . I was to go once a week for eight successive weeks, and this short span of time meant, of course, that the seeds had to be chosen carefully, so that the children could see the results. I could think of no flowers that would grow and bloom in eight weeks. I ordered onion sets, carrots, radishes, beans, lettuce, pumpkin, cucumbers, and zuccini squash.

separated them into two groups and I took the younger ones first, wishing to goodness I could teach one at a time and do it properly.

We divided half the garden plot into five sections and each child put his or her name on a marker and staked out a claim. They pulled back the hay and made rows, crooked, of course, but there was no time to fuss about that; the seeds had all to be planted that first day, since the growing season for them was going to be so short, and I was naturally more than anxious for the young gardeners to see some real results.

They got the carrots in, and radishes planted on top of them, then other rows of lettuce and string beans. When that was done, each child planted two hills of pumpkins and two of cucumbers, and two zuccini squash.

My main worry was that they would put the smaller seeds in too deeply, although I kept warning them about this, and dashed from one to the other. I also was afraid they would never find the crooked rows, and to guard against that calamity, I sent one of the boys to the house for a newspaper which we tore into strips, then placed over the planted seeds. The strips were held down with hay.

I went through the same performance with the second group, with two improvements: these children were older and, also, I was by this time an experienced teacher of gardening to small amateurs. After the seeds were all planted, there was nothing more to do that day except pray that at least a few of them would struggle through. Before I left for home, I asked Mrs. Doherty to remind the children that I had cautioned them to be sure to look under the strips on Friday (this was Tuesday) to see if any sprouts were showing, and if so, to remove the paper.

Later that day Fred came up to me in the yard and said: "Mrs. Doherty just telephoned. You're fired."

"I'm not surprised," I replied, although I was, a little; it seemed premature.

Fred laughed and continued: "She just wanted to tell you the children talked of nothing but their gardens all through lunch."

I liked that, naturally. Then on Friday Mrs. Doherty called again to say that the children had removed the strips of paper because absolutely everything was up. She said the children were excited about it all, and that the beans were two inches high, which I had some difficulty believing.

But when I went over the following Tuesday, I found she hadn't exaggerated; I had never seen a week-old garden so flourishing. Obviously it was wonderful soil; what a piece of luck for beginners, not to mention me!

The first group proudly showed me their plants, then I ran into a snag I should have foreseen: although the seeds had come up profusely, the plants were still too small to be thinned, and in a well-mulched garden thinning is, after the planting, the only other job until time to harvest. There was nothing for the children to do.

In some desperation I sent them for more hay, and could have wept at the speed with which they brought it and put it between the rows. And this was really bad tactics, because it was unnecessary, and one of the main points of mulch gardening is that there is almost no work attached; I was giving the children the wrong impression.

The previous week I had had them plant onion sets in flower pots and I now managed to kill a little time admiring those. Then I got the idea of having them plant some more sets as I do—just throw them on top of the ground and toss hay on them.

By the time the second group showed up, I had thought of something else: I had them each put in some additional seeds which weren't to be mulched. First, they had to spade, and I made a big to-do about the great advantages of never having to plow or spade your garden if you kept it mulched from year to year. This other method would require cultivating and weeding, and also watering, if rain was scarce. And I figured that thus the good features of mulch-gardening would sink in. But primarily I had in mind that each time I went from now on, there would be some work for at least the older children to do in their unmulched part.

The third week the younger group thinned their plants a little, then, after half-an-hour, I gave up and dismissed them. When the second group appeared I felt easy; the unmulched plots had weeds in them which would have to be pulled or hoed.

But Richard outwitted me; he had learned the mulch lesson too well. He asked: "What do we hoe for? Why can't we just get more hay and put it on top of the weeds?"

Well, they could, of course, and did, which took only about ten minutes; thus my hope of having some work to occupy them was defeated. I was licked, and that evening I called Mrs. Doherty; I said she would be wasting money and I would be wasting time if I went over there and just stood around, racking my brain. But she was against my quitting; she said the children looked forward all week to showing me how their plants had grown.

So I gave in, and at the next session we had a fine time: the children liked to swing me and I loved it, and they showed me the horse, and the puppets they had made, and what they had done in the art class.

The fifth week we sat under a pear tree and told stories. I tried at first to more or less confine them to garden happenings but we got completely off the subject and stayed off.

We did some thinning the next week, and the children stuffed little radishes, dirt and all, into my mouth as well as their own; they also ate lettuce from their patch. Then we flocked to the swimming pool.

The seventh visit was chiefly occupied with eating raw beans, cucumbers, and zuccini from the youngsters' gardens, and the eighth week some newspaper took pictures of all of the school's activities. But Ed Lang was also there with his camera and concentrated on anything which illustrated the easy life of mulch-gardeners—swimming, swinging, lying under a tree.

8

A strawberry, corn and potato rotation—with comments on witch grass

This chapter is confined to things which people have told me or written me, and also to quotations from articles I have read. I don't feel that I need explain why Professor Richard Clemence steals the show, nor apologize for letting him; I think the reason will be obvious.

In that first garden book I said that somebody should try throwing mulch on top of sod to find out how soon one could plant in such a spot without plowing. Well, of course Dick had done this and he reports: "On most new ground, a few inches of hay in the fall will make it possible to plant any kind of crop the following year without disturbing the sod. With the Stout System, spading, plowing, and cultivating are all unnecessary, and do more harm than good. If a heavy hay cover is laid on even the toughest sod in the summer, plantings can be made through it the following spring. No other preparation of the soil is required."

He wrote me later about this: "I was careful to say on 'most' new ground, partly because I have not started gardens on clay, and partly because I had the question of witch grass in mind."

In the first chapter of this book, when I was trying to answer the various questions I have been asked, I said that the amount of lime one should use had nothing to do with mulching; that is, do as you always have; if you have reason to believe that your soil is too acid, act accordingly. But now listen to Dick:

"If you use the hay mulch continuously for a number of years, you can practically forget all about acid or alkaline soil problems—along with dusting and spraying and the use of chemical fertilizers and 'soil conditioners.' I grow everything from beets to blueberries under the Stout System, and pay no attention to acidity or alkalinity any more. My experience has been that ample organic matter acts as an effective buffer and helps to neutralize extremes of pH in any soil."

Later, in a letter to me, he wrote further about this: "On acidity, alkalinity, and soil testing in general, I am inclined to speak with caution. I have not much to go on besides my own personal experience, and that is an inadequate basis for any very positive statements. What I do mean to do is to question the validity of the whole business. I can see why dead dirt is unable to support vegetation without all sorts of special treatment. Flocculation must be promoted, locked-up nutrients released, and doubtless a dozen other things like adding trace elements, would improve matters. But it does not seem to me that many of these practices are relevant to genuine soil that is full of life. Its physical condition leaves small room for improvement, and how any nutrients can be 'locked up' in it, I do not see. My guess is that most of the conversation about pH reflects the 'progress' of our agricultural science in the wake of the diminishing organic content of our commercial farms. Certainly many of the best farmers in other parts of the world are proceeding admirably in complete ignorance of it."

Since I never had been able to make up my mind about what was the best use to make of wood ashes, I included that question along with dozens of others which I asked Dick from time to time. He replied:

"I should not question the desirability of using wood ashes as a fertilizer. They are a free source of potash, and should do more good than harm, unless the lye that leaches from them is fatal to soil organisms. I simply do not know about that. I do know, though, that wood ashes make an effective deterrent to cucumber beetles, squash bugs, and vine borers that come over from your neighbors' gardens to attack yours at times. Shaken liberally over the vines when the leaves are wet, the ashes will discourage these pests without much cost to anyone." Later, my brother Rex told me to put wood ashes around anything which needed a good strong stalk, so I'm now giving them to the corn.

Now here is a little gem which I haven't tried. Dick writes: "After trying many ways of disposing of corn stalks, ranging from composting to chopping and spreading, I have arrived at a nearly ideal scheme. As soon as the corn is harvested, I flatten the stalks to the ground by bending them over and stamping on them. Then I cover the flattened mess with hay. In the spring, any kind of plants can be set with a trowel through this cover. By spreading a little compost, loam or peat moss on top, even small seeds can be started, and the roots will penetrate into the decaying mass below. The results are astonishing to anyone who has not tried the method, and the work is reduced to almost nothing. I should add that I am not troubled with corn borers at all, and of course use no sprays or dusts of any kind."

Last winter, Dick told me that in hot weather lettuce seed is sometimes cooled in the refrigerator overnight before planting because it germinates better in cold ground than in warm and this way one can at least have the seeds cold. So a few weeks ago (in July) I put some seeds in the freezer and also filled some trays with water and froze that. The next morning I planted the seed, covered it with blocks of ice and put paper and feed bags over it. The seed germinated in two and a half days, Now and then I put ice cubes between the rows and keep it shaded. So far, the lettuce is doing as well as it does in early spring.

Dick has this to say in an article in *Organic Gardening & Farming:* "Perhaps my application of the Stout System to a rotation of strawberries, corn and potatoes would be of interest to other readers. These three crops all present special problems, because they ordinarily require so much space. For the back-yard gardener to manage all of them is usually out of the question, and I have experimented for many years in an effort to solve the problem.

"Since this method is a rotation, we may begin at any stage of it, so let us start with the strawberries. I will try to show how some of the ideas I have already mentioned apply in this scheme. Let me say at this point that I have eaten strawberries prepared in every way I could think of, and that my notion of perfection is to pick the berries dead ripe after the sun has evaporated excess moisture, and eat them immediately when they are still warm, but swimming in heavy chilled cream. If you have not tried organically grown strawberries this way, you may still be wondering if they are worth the time and trouble they require.

"Now for the rotation. I set a new bed every year, buying 100 virus-free plants, and spacing them in four rows one foot apart, with the plants also one foot apart in the rows. The plants are set through a thin mulch left from the previous season, and more hay is added as growth occurs, and as weeds need to be smothered. Since I want results, not only on the strawberries but on the corn to follow, I spread 100 pounds of Bovung and 50 pounds of bone meal over the bed as soon as the plants are well started. I remove all runners the first year, which sounds like a lot of work. Actually, however, it takes about ten minutes a week. A walk down each side of the bed, with a pair of grass shears in hand, will take care of the runners about as quickly as you would ordinarily inspect the plants anyway.

"As early as possible the following spring, before the strawberry plants are getting into full leaf, I seed sweet corn between the rows and along each side of the bed. A string keeps the corn rows straight, and I push the kernels into the ground with my fingers, spacing them closely, and taking account of the way the strawberry plants are developing. When the berries are ready to pick in June, the corn should be four or five inches high, and easy to avoid in the harvesting. The corn should be an early and strong-growing variety. I have had the best luck with North Star and Golden Beauty, but others may be equally good. I count on the five

25-plant rows of corn to yield at least fifteen dozen fine ears, and have not been disappointed yet. While the corn is growing it needs no attention at all. The strawberry plants continue to live and to shade the corn roots, and the corn thrives on the extra Bovung and bone meal applied earlier.

"After the corn has all been harvested, the stalks are simply flattened to the ground over the surviving strawberry plants and covered with several inches of hay. The following spring, potatoes are laid on top of whatever remains of all this, and mulched with a heavy hay blanket. Again, nothing remains to be done but to gather potatoes as they are wanted. According to the chemical school, everything should be riddled by insects and diseases, but I have barely enough evidence of these to realize what is supposed to be destroying my crops. I harvest all my potatoes with my bare hands, because it is so satisfying to handle the living soil and to discover one handsome tuber after another growing in it. The potato harvest thus leaves the whole space in perfect condition for the next crop. I merely cover the ground with hay, and wait for my strawberry plants to arrive."

And now to that Number One Enemy—witch grass. Or, according to what part of the country you live in, you may call it Bermuda, or nut, or Johnson grass. I have had letters asking about all of these, and from descriptions of the way they behave, I've concluded that they are what we call witch grass here in Connecticut or at least are closely related. They have a thick white root which creeps and spreads rapidly, somewhat the way asparagus does. I have talked and written so much, and so feelingly, about this pest that instead of just repeating myself, I'm going to quote Dick again. Early in 1959 he wrote me:

"Fortunately, witch grass is comparatively rare, but where it exists, it is certainly in a class by itself. Some twenty years ago I was gardening on a place completely covered with the stuff, and have since wished that I had taken time out for more experiments. I did conduct a fair number, but all of them were tests of the recommendations of the 'authorities,' and every one was a failure. My provisional conclusion was that witch grass must be dug out with a spading fork inch by inch by the gardener in person (no one else can possibly acquire the necessary incentive), digging the full depth of the tines, and calculating progress by the square foot. If this is done over the whole garden area, and if a two-foot border is left around it to be gone

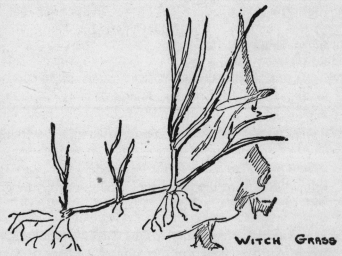

WITCH GRASS

. . . And now to that Number One Enemy—Witch grass. Or, according to what part of the country you live in you may call it Bermuda, or Nut, or Johnson grass. I have had letters asking about all of these, and from descriptions of the way they behave, I've concluded that they are what we call Witch grass here in Connecticut. . . . .

over again each year, witch grass can be successfully 'controlled.' Or at least it can be kept out of your garden. I have found no way to control any that is in it. The stolons will go through potatoes or any other kind of root crop, and I have seen them doing well in what I had supposed was solid cement."

Then in August I got the following letter from him:

"This is just an interim report on the progress of my current experiment with witch grass. You will remember that I saved a patch to run tests on when you told me about yours.

"Before trying anything, I pondered the problem at length, and gave special attention to the failures I always had years ago. The hypothesis I finally decided to test was that the underground stems could not continue to develop if no green leaves were feeding the rest of the system. Heretofore, I had been trying to keep the stems from getting leaves to the surface, but this will not work, as you know. This time, I reasoned that the thing to do might be to begin by covering the flourishing leaves with hay enough to kill them, wait for more leaves to emerge, kill these, and so on, until no more leaves appeared.

"In order to give the witch grass a strong start, I waited until June before first spreading the hay, and began with grass more than six inches tall. I flattened this as I spread the hay over it, and ended with some three inches of hay cover. By early July, some new leaves were making their appearance, and I added another inch of hay. I have done this once since, and only a few spears are now starting to show. I shall smother these shortly, but it looks to me as if the performance is getting real results. The crucial test, I suppose, will come next spring, and perhaps the whole patch will then be as green as ever. But if not, there is going to be a better solution to the witch-grass problem than any I have heard of yet, and I am hopeful enough at the prospect to tell you about it now."

After I got this letter I naturally rushed out and tossed hay on some witch grass, of which I have plenty. When it began to show through in spots I put on more, but in the iris bed, where I didn't want to smother the plants, I simply lifted the hay and tucked the green grass shoots back under. I asked Dick if it was all right to do that, and he said yes; so it must be.

Although I can't assure you at this stage that Dick has found the weapon which will defeat this enemy, I really believe he has. Perhaps you will try it out yourself, and if it does the trick, we can assume that the same procedure will solve the problem of the other few things that come up through mulch and drive us crazy, such as wild morning-glories, vetch and sour grass.

I read recently that in Missouri the farmers rent geese during the cotton-growing season because geese eat Johnson grass. I'm also told that black plastic kills this grass and that's fine, but if I had put it, for instance, all over the iris bed, I would have killed the flowers. Too, it's expensive and extra work, while, if you are going to mulch your garden with hay anyway, killing the witch grass in the process is simply a by-product. Also, you can go ahead with your gardening instead of having to temporarily abandon it while the plastic is doing the job of killing the grass.

Here's a slight variation which I'm trying. Witch grass surrounds my plot almost entirely, and up to now I've kept a small trench around the patch to keep the grass from creeping in. Instead of wasting any more time digging, or using up a lot of hay out there, I have made a wide path all around my plot of thick layers of newspapers and magazines, covering them with cardboard from large cartons. I can keep widening the path as I get one strip under control. Thus I don't waste hay, and more important I can do the job in cold weather, when I'm in need of out-door exercise; the baled hay is frozen in winter and I can't handle it. I've roughly figured out that the very last of the witch grass and I will just about simultaneously give up the ghost.

I asked you not to make your planting diagram until you had read this chapter, because last winter Dick came up with the kind of idea which is so sensible and obvious that it makes one mutter: why on earth didn't I think of that? Instead of making a thin row of carrots, beets and so on, he scatters his seeds over a space a foot wide. Instead of long rows of things, with paths in between them which take up a lot of room, he has short wide rows. It's obvious that it will work, for that's exactly what an annual flower bed is—a lot of plants the same distance apart in all directions, not in thin widely-spaced rows.

In these broad rows Dick scatters the seed right on the surface of the ground, shakes fine peat moss on them, walks firmly on the mixture of seeds and moss, then wets the row thoroughly with a hose.

Early this spring I planted wide rows of lettuce and spinach as Dick suggested, but because watering anything off there in my plot is somewhat laborious, I proceeded a little differently—pulling back the mulch, marking the wide row, scattering the seeds, then, without covering them at all, I firmly walked on them. But then for a month we had no rain which made me realize that if we had a long dry spell, I would have no way to mulch close to the plants and conserve the moisture. So, later, when I planted other things such as carrots and beets, I still kept to the wide-row idea, but instead of broadcasting the seeds, I planted a few thin rows, three or four inches apart. I tucked mulch in between these narrowly-spaced rows.

John Lorenz thinks that all this is a good idea, but he says that the tiny shoots will be very tender and without roots, since they are planted on top of the ground, and that if we have a hot dry day or two when they first come up, I might well lose the whole business. So we decided it would be sensible to lightly sprinkle some hay over the newly-uncovered sprouts, to give them a little shade, which I did.

With three cheers for Professor Clemence, let's now turn our attention to some other friends who have lent a helping hand. Here's a letter from Hester Sprague, Rocky River, Ohio, who came to see my gardening method last August; then we met again a month later in Columbus, Ohio, where I gave a talk at the Natural Food Associates Convention. She told me about some innovations of hers and I asked her to please write it all out and mail it to me. Which she did, telling me to put it in "the correct sentence form" but I see nothing wrong with her form, so here it is as she wrote it:

"Using a bed for carrots instead of rows, rake a spot two feet wide and as long as you want, early in the spring (before the weeds start to germinate). Broadcast carrots as thin as you can and cover with one/half to three/fourths inches of sawdust. I use any kind that I happen to have. A few weeds will come up but if your land has been mulched for a long time it is quite free of weeds. (At least, I've found that to be true.) These few weeds can easily be pulled if and when you might need to thin the carrots. Experience being the greatest teacher, I've found that by taking a pinch of carrot seeds and standing upright, then dropping it, they scatter and are not too thick to produce nicely. Beets may be done in the same manner. Use three/fourths to one inch of sawdust."

This ties right in with Dick's ideas of surface planting and wide rows. The difference is in the rather deep covering Mrs. Sprague uses. She goes on:

"Being very lazy (I hope only in the garden department) I knock the bottoms out of cantaloupe crates and set them over my tomatoes when the plants are small and then I never have to bother to keep up with the tying of new growth. The plants just drape themselves over the crates, but this year I had to use crates on the outside of the originals as my plants grew so large. Borage planted with tomatoes seems to call the bees and I had sets on the very first blossoms, which most always fall off unset. Borage has a heavenly blue flower on it and is bushy, about two feet high and the same in diameter. My first year I made a mistake of planting the borage so thick that I could hardly get to my tomatoes. Live and learn! I also use gallon glass jugs with the bottoms off to put over my tomato plants when I get them out early in the season (here the first of May)."

A letter from Mrs. Elliott in West Virginia may be of help:

"After reading your book we tried your mulch-type-garden last year. We raised lots of peas and beans. . . . After some experimentation we now make rows in the mulch (applied in the fall) with a tool used in making cement. The tool resembles a straightened out hoe, and should be kept quite sharp. With this 'chopper' we cut through the mulch, and about an inch into the soil, a little sideways motion with the handle, and thus we have a sort of narrow trench, into which we drop such seeds as beans, peas, corn, etc. That is all there is to it until harvesting. Also, we have a post-hole-digging tool called a spud, to make holes for tomato plants. Your method saves a lot of hard work."

And here is something by E. T. Latting in the *Rural New Yorker* which was a real pleasure to read: "Slugs and 'pill bugs' are plentiful, but they prefer the rotting vegetation to the live plants; they feed on the old leaves, breaking them down for incorporation into the soil."

I hear you protesting that slugs do eat your live plants, and I believe you, but maybe you didn't give them enough old leaves to eat. And maybe they would have eaten even more live plants if you hadn't had some mulch there for them. In other words, nobody has so far convinced me that slugs are a bigger menace when one mulches than when one doesn't.

We now come to the problem of a heavy clay soil, about which I know nothing from experience, and neither, unfortunately, does Professor Clemence. (I suppose he wouldn't thank me for that "unfortunately"; who wants to struggle with hardpan?) But many people have told me of the progress they have made; Mrs. John Reilly of Shelton, Conn. wrote:

"Following the method outlined in your book I covered a plot of hard, cement-like soil with hay. Short of hay, the rest of the garden remained uncovered and you should see the difference! Always before, this soil had to be broken with a pick and grub-hoe, nothing else would do it; now the mulched half is soft, moist and friable. For the first time in fifteen years we had peas. I have planted peas each year without success, and this year, an unfavorable one, I had peas to eat and freeze."

And E. W. Morse says in the *Rural New Yorker:* "Before

mulching, my garden consisted of six inches of depleted top soil over 85 feet of hardpan. Witch grass and pigweed grew profusely; there was no end to hand weeding and cultivating. The ground was so wet and sticky that it could not be plowed before the middle of May. Early plantings were impossible. Each dry spell baked the earth almost like brick; earthworms did not, and could not, exist.

"Three years ago, after the crops were up, I started mulching with two inches of baled hay. During the Summer, I threw more hay on bare spots and weed patches; pea pods, vines and corn husks were added to the mulch. In late Fall I spread an additional two inches of hay over the entire garden. The result was spectacular. The following Spring the soil was ready for planting the middle of April. Raking aside the remaining thin layer of unrotted mulch was no problem at all.

"Since then we have not plowed, harrowed or cultivated. Best of all, the top soil, becoming deeper and richer, now matures two ears of corn to a stalk."

Over and over, in this problem of clay soil, I have been told that the thing to do is to dig in plenty of humus of all kinds, also sand. When I talked to a gathering of fifteen hundred people a few months ago someone (as always) asked what to do with a heavy soil, and I requested help from the audience on it, and I also reported what others had told me about it.

After the meeting a woman came up to me and said that she and her husband had been struggling with a garden "like cement." They decided to try my system but before they did, they plowed (or spaded) under a large amount of sand, sawdust, manure, leaves, hay, and corncobs. She said the result amazed them, even though they had hopefully expected a good deal. I was indeed sorry that she hadn't got up and told this to that big audience, but apparently she was too modest and timid.

There are many others who have helped me in various ways—far too many to mention. I suppose that most of us are human enough to enjoy a little recognition and thanks for the services we render, and I am very sorry that I can't here, publicly, call the honor roll and present a gold star to each of you. Your suggestions, the reports of your successes (and even failures) are all helpful.

I am especially grateful to those of you who take the trouble to spread the good word, who persuade the local library to handle my books, and who give talks to your garden clubs about the system, or merely tell the neighbors about it. One very busy man takes the trouble to write articles about it for various magazines and farm papers; others write letters to the periodicals they read.

All this means more to me than I could even begin to tell you. In my early childhood I had some kind of vague yearning to Save the World from something or other; now all I ask is to save a small part of it from over-working in the effort to produce things that are good to eat or are lovely to see. Which is modest enough, I guess, and realistic, since it is no doubt all I'll get, no matter what I might ask.

If my head was still in those clouds of my youth, I suppose that besides wanting to save the world, I would now throw in the moon.

. . . . . *In my early childhood I had some kind of vague yearning to Save the World from something or other:*

9

Flowers and mulch

I am unobservant but I never miss seeing something which really appeals to me. I love cats and when I walk into a yard or house where one is around, I always know it, while dogs can abound without my realizing it until they begin barking and jumping on me and licking me and tearing my stockings. And I could go into a room with a big pile of fine vegetables lying on a table in front of me and not notice them, but if even one flower is around in a vase, or a pot, I am drawn to it as by a magnet.

So why, beyond the practical reason, do I spend a great deal more time growing vegetables than I do flowers, and even enjoy it more? I don't know, and, anyway, does anyone care?

I have been told that garden clubs would stop asking me to give talks when they found out that I couldn't seem to resist discussing growing vegetables. That hasn't happened, although it's true that almost without exception the clubs who have asked me to talk to them about my method are made up of people who are interested primarily in flowers. Since there's no need to encourage them on that score, I just go ahead and talk about vegetables, and when they find out how little work there is to producing them with my system, many of them probably begin to grow them.

Sometimes, when I know that a group I am about to address goes in almost exclusively for flowers, I start out by asking how many have a vegetable garden, and perhaps only two or three hands go up. But I boldly say that I think I will tell them a little about how I grow vegetables, and that my method also applies to flowers. After a brief discussion of both, I ask for questions, and it is gratifying to find that I seem to have already interested a big percentage of them in starting a vegetable patch; my explanation had shown them how little work was involved in being able to go out to one's own patch and pick fresh lettuce, asparagus, parsley, and so on.

Why am I making a case for vegetables in the flower chapter? Because I want you to remember that in general the things I say about one also apply to the other. In this chapter I will assume that you realize you can follow the same procedure, as far as no-digging and mulching goes, as is described through the rest of the book.

I think I will begin with house plants; I know so little about them, and have so few, that I can dispose of them in a hurry. Did you ever try potting a petunia plant in the fall? I know a woman who does this and they bloom for her all winter. A year ago my sister and I tried it but we had no luck at all; we thought that perhaps it was because ours were hybrids. Recently (in October) we potted three of the every-day kind which seem to be thriving and may mean business. Although I doubt it; my main trouble with house plants is that we have so few sunny windows.

About African violets, I have nothing to add to what I said in my other book, which was that they bloom if they please, and don't if they don't feel like it, and why don't we all relax? If any psychologist ever takes time to find what motivates people who have, say, eighty African violet plants instead of being content with eight, I hope he will let me in on the secret. However hard I try, I can't figure it out and I haven't found any such addict who has been able to give me a reason which makes sense to me.

But what did I say—eighty? Just the other day I read of a woman who has twelve hundred African violet plants, and when asked why so many, she said it was a compulsion. Well, she at least apparently doesn't need a psychiatrist to figure out what her trouble is. I can understand why people keep writing books about this flower; why not, if they can get someone to publish them? But I can't grasp why anyone reads them.

Do you have an oxalis plant? I have one in an ordinary

flower pot with a wire fastened around it, and there it hangs on a hook all winter in our south kitchen window, so unassuming and cheerful and responsive that I would be sorry to be without it. I set it out of doors in the summer, and in the fall divide it into several plants.

This past year it was especially ambitious and presented me with seven new growths. You don't need to hesitate to pot the tiniest bulb or smallest bit of root, for although they may look as though they could never amount to anything, they begin to make new leaves in an incredibly short time and are soon in flower. My sister prefers to take one or two of those which seem least likely to do anything over to her cottage; it's interesting to watch their unfailing and energetic performance. I was recently told they can be grown out-of-doors; so I planted some in a sheltered spot out of doors last fall and they wintered over beautifully.

I have written so much about gardenias that I have little to add here. From my experience and observation, it seems to me they are richly endowed with the will to live and ask for very little. Yet we are told that only a few of the many thousands, which are bought every year around Easter, survive.

These plants are, I suppose, forced, and when they are taken from their environment and the "treatment" (whatever it is) is discontinued, they apparently have trouble adjusting to new conditions. I have been loaned a few such plants, the purpose being to find out whether I can save them. It can be done; all it takes is patience, lots of water, little sun. And perhaps I should add: no fussing, no adding of this or trying that. These plants aren't sick, they're just disgusted with all the unnecessary dosing and anxiety.

My largest gardenia, the mother of the many small ones I have given to friends, finally died at the age of nineteen years. By then it was producing about two hundred blossoms a year and was a great pleasure, but it had some drawbacks. We had finally been obliged to put it in a big tub and the whole thing was so heavy that Fred and I couldn't carry it in and out of the house in fall and spring; we had to rely on friends or neighbors to help with it.

It finally began to drop its leaves, not normally as it always had in autumn when first taken back into the house, but so many of them that there was obviously something wrong. John Lorenz (who had given it to me) looked it over and found nothing which explained the way it was acting. It was a depressing sight, and it sat in the west window where I had to face it three times a day at meals. Having heard that it's important for one to feel cheerful while eating I decided this couldn't go on; my own health was more important than the gardenia's. And besides, if I died first who was going to take care of it?

There was another angle: from all appearances it was going to give up, and how could I, who had written reams about how to grow gardenias, admit that this spectacular plant which I had talked so much about had died and I didn't know why? There seemed to be only one thing to do: put it out on the porch where, for one thing, it would be out of my sight, and for another, it would no doubt freeze.

We put it out and it did freeze, and I didn't have to expose my ignorance if I didn't want to. When anyone asked me what had happened to the large gardenia, I could just look sad and say it had frozen, since I wasn't under oath and didn't have to tell "the whole truth."

Speaking of being ruthlessly put out on a porch and left to freeze to death, the story of my camellia is apropos. About seven years ago Rex gave me a fine one, saying: "You're one of the few people I know whose gardenias' buds don't drop off. If you can make this camellia hang on to its blossoms until they open, you're a genius."

Well, it turned out I wasn't a genius. The plant remained healthy, grew perhaps normally (I don't know what normal growth is for a camellia), but the buds dropped off year after year. I don't go for house plants that don't behave, and

I wouldn't be afraid to bet that I'm the world's worst nurse, which includes the care of ailing plants and animals. So I was looking around for someone to wish this camellia on, and in the meantime I complained about it in my weekly garden column.

A woman (who doesn't want her name mentioned) asked to borrow it for a year and I gladly handed it over; the following spring she brought it back, now a large thriving plant simply reeking with buds and blossoms. She told me the various things she had done for it but the only one that really interested me was that it had spent the winter in a room where the temperature never rose above fifty degrees.

I had already strongly suspected that a too-warm-room was the secret of the buds dropping, for the only two blooming camellia plants I knew about were owned by people who kept them in a very cool room. Since I had no such favorable spot I saw no hope of my having any success with the plant, so, partly for that reason and partly because I felt this woman had earned it, I tried to get her to keep it, but she firmly refused.

It sat in the yard all summer and thrived, and I experimentally left it out through several light frosts. Then, in November I put it on the porch and left it there all winter, which wasn't entirely a case of my being hardhearted, although I did say to it: now you do just as you please—sink or swim. I did have some faint hope that it might survive, for I had been hearing vague rumors to the effect that some camellias, if protected, may be left out all winter even in a cold climate.

When the weather began to get really wintry I got a little nervous and moved the plant away from the window (our porch is glassed-in but unheated) and over against the wall of the house. And Fred put a thermometer close by it so that in case it did pull through we would know what it could stand. (I suppose I could have wrapped it in a gunny sack or something but I didn't.)

Fred goes to bed later than I do, and on very cold nights he would check the thermometer just before he went up-stairs; the coldest he saw it was fifteen above zero, but it probably went lower than that later on in the night. I kept the plant watered which meant that most of the time the poor thing was sitting in ice.

It lived. When we put it out on the porch in November it was full of buds, some of them almost half-open and showing color, and these stayed exactly at that point until early spring, when we put the plant in the yard again; then they all opened up.

That was this last spring. I am writing this in late November, and the camellia is now heavy with buds again. But they are still small and I'm sure they won't even begin to open before really cold weather sets in. Soon the plant will again be put in the porch; this time I have no qualms about it.

Just as there are women who are born nurses—good at the job and love it—there are also people who have a liking and talent for bringing sick plants back to health. So what few house plants I have are always in fine shape; if they aren't I give them to some expert nurse for her enjoyment in rescuing them.

A summer or two ago a woman telephoned me to say that some group she belonged to (not a garden club) would like to come and see my rose garden; there would be about forty of them. I don't like to seem unfriendly so I said for them to come ahead if they wanted to, but I thought it was only fair to say beforehand that I had only eight or nine rosebushes and they all looked terrible. Obviously she had me confused with someone else. I told her why people flocked here to have a look at my garden, and she decided that her crowd would like to come anyway, which they did, and I feel sure that at least some of them got interested in growing their own vegetables.

But about roses. If you are growing them, and are satisfied with the results, you will be just as well off to skip the next few paragraphs. And if you *aren't* happy about yours, you too will be better off if you skip, for anything I say will probably only make you unhappier.

Now and then I hear of someone who grows "wonderful" roses, free of Black Leaf Spot, and which bloom all summer. I've never seen such a rose garden, and even if I could have one *only* if I sprayed it, I wouldn't pay that price. For one thing, I understand that this business of spraying has to be done quite often, and at certain times.

I have many things to do, some of which I am obliged to do in order to keep up my end in this business of daily living. But much that I do (this includes growing our vegetables) is done because I want to and enjoy it. I like to keep those two reasons for all my activities in a nice balance. If I deliberately and unnecessarily added a job here and there which I felt I *must* do, and particularly things which had to be done at certain times, I would soon begin to feel pushed and ordered around and hectic. I don't like roses well enough to become a slave to them; there are many lovely flowers one can grow which are relatively undemanding.

That isn't all of it. I don't believe in spraying, and I'm not talking only about the squirting of poison on vegetables we expect to eat. I am against poisoning our little enemies if at the same time I must kill any of our little friends, such as bees, which might happen to be in the vicinity. As one man put it: what would we think of a general who ordered his soldiers to fire on everybody, including his own troops?

So I decided to give up the few hybrid tea-roses I had, and started by giving two of them away. Then came that winter which killed so many things in this vicinity and it took some of my bushes. So I have only two left, a Peace and an Eclipse and I will probably give those to some unenlightened person who doesn't know better than to accept them.

But I do have a Rose Hugonis which doesn't get leaf spot and is lovely. And a well-behaved New Dawn (a climber) which is perhaps my favorite rose.

Do anybody's bushes have roses all summer and fall? I don't think so. It seems to me that our attitude to roses is too much like our feeling about our friends: we are likely to expect too much from them. If we like half-a-dozen things about a person, why do we feel that he should have seven traits that appeal to us? If he's a pleasant addition to a dinner party, must he also be the sort of person who arrives on time? Or helps with the dishes?

And it's the same with roses. They don't have everything, and just because the people who sell them like to say they are ever-blooming, are we obliged to believe it? Because people sell sprays to do away with Black Leaf Spot, do we have to keep on using them even if we find out they don't do what they're supposed to?

What's wrong with being realistic? We don't expect peonies or lilacs to bloom right through until frost and we're not likely to expect them to unless someone gets the bright idea of advertising them as ever-blooming; then what a tizzy we'll be in, feeling as frustrated over them as we now are over roses!

Is it the fault of the roses that we expect more from them than they have to give? Someone said to me: "I like iris because, unlike roses, when they're through blooming, that's it. They don't try to kid you."

True enough, and roses don't try to fool us either; is it their fault if we are masters at kidding ourselves? And speaking of false claims, we don't have to believe advertisers when, in autumn, they tell us that right then is the very best time to plant roses. It's understandable that the people who handle plants would like to sell them at once, and they don't much mind what they say if they can get you to buy them. In my experience roses do equally well whether planted in spring or fall, so if you want to wait, do so; when spring comes the advertisements will be saying that NOW is the time to plant roses.

At a guess we have about forty peony bushes and, guessing again, I probably spend not more than two hours a year caring for them. I never remove the tops, not even in spring when they are dead; they lie there and add to the mulch, and the new plants grow so rapidly and luxuriantly that they soon hide anything beneath them that's unsightly. Mulching the plants is also no work; leaves blow against the bushes in the fall, are caught there and stay, rotting and enriching the soil.

I am willing to concede that I may spend as much as half-an-hour a year at the tossing of some leaves or a bit of hay on a weed that has come through, but no more time than that. The rest of the estimated two hours devoted to peonies is spent in picking them, either for our living room or to give away. And later cutting off the ones that have died on the bush; these are left on the ground where they fall.

About four years ago a woman who called here to see my gardening system and who obviously knew a great deal more about growing flowers than I did, admired my peony bushes and asked if I ever had some disease or other (I forget what she called it) on the leaves. I had never heard of this but could tell by her expression when she spoke of it that it was highly undesirable. I said I didn't think I had

A woman who called to see my gardening system, and who obviously knew a great deal more about growing flowers than I did, admired my peony bushes and asked if I ever had some disease (I forget what she called it) on the leaves. I had never heard of it, but could tell by her expression that it was highly undesirable. I said I didn't think I had ever seen it on the plants; then as we walked along she pounced on a leaf and said there it was, ...

ever seen it on the plants, then as we walked along she pounced on a leaf and said there it was. She warned me to watch carefully, and whenever I saw an affected leaf, I should take it off and be sure to burn it; otherwise, I would lose all my bushes.

Well, I sort of forgot the whole thing. Probably my underlying feeling was that I didn't intend to be bossed around by peonies any more than by roses. Which may sound a bit on the stupid side, so in my defense I will add that I might have followed the woman's instructions if I had been convinced she was right. But the truth was that by now I had little reason to feel sure that anyone was right, including myself.

So I turned my attention to other activities. Then one day late in summer I discovered that most of the peony leaves were turning black, and so I thought: goodby peonies, maybe. The outcome? Every spring since then my bushes have looked fine and healthy and have produced hundreds of blossoms.

In late August last year a man and woman (from Pennsylvania, I think) called here to look over the garden, and when the man saw that the peony bushes, which are out by the barn in full sun, looked almost dead, he asked me what was wrong. I said I guessed that nothing was. He began questioning me, and told me with great positiveness that this happened because I didn't cut the tops off in the fall.

Among a few trifles which I have learned in a long lifetime one is not to waste my breath, so I meekly said nothing, and we walked on across the yard and came to other peony plants which were green and luxuriant.

"Ah, you do cut these tops off," exclaimed my informant, and I replied: "No, I don't cut off any of them."

He was puzzled and finally decided that the partial shade, which these green bushes were in, made the difference. Some people simply have to know why, even if the answer is wrong. However, I'm not saying that this last guess of his wasn't right; I rather suspect it was.

We have three holly bushes which we bought from Earl Dilatush, Route 25, Robbinsville, New Jersey, and I keep wood chips around them for a mulch but give them no special protection in winter; many visitors are surprised that they live in this cold climate but so far ours have done all right. Obviously, Mr. Dilatush's plants are hardy in the North. This past spring, after a winter which killed several of our rosebushes, the two smallest hollies looked completely gone, and perhaps anyone but a confirmed optimist would have dug them up. They lost every leaf, but before long began to show some green and soon were thriving again.

There are two syringa (or mock orange) bushes in our yard, one with fragrance, one without. The former makes a relatively small bush, then stops, while the latter grows quite rapidly and gets large and tall. Some people don't know that there are these two varieties and may be disappointed if they are buying one chiefly for the fragrance. Also, if they are acquainted only with the small variety they may be put out if they inadvertently plant the other kind, then find they have a tree on their hands in an inconvenient spot.

I know some gardeners who have given up trying to have crocuses because rabbits get them before they have a chance to bloom. If you care enough you can easily protect them by bending a long piece of hardware cloth (any width you find convenient) in the middle, thus making a long tent for your crocuses. After they begin blooming you can of course keep the tent tipped over, so that you can enjoy them when you're around, then cover them again toward evening, when the rabbits might *like* to enjoy them.

I have very little to tell about annuals; I do have a new little trick in planting zinnias, which also applies to anything (flower or vegetable) which I grow from seed and space a foot or two apart.

I grow zinnias in the tulip row, planting three or four seeds about a foot apart. I used to mark the spots with sticks but I've improved on this: I put a berry box on top of each planting; a stone, bit of dirt, or mulch, will keep the box from blowing away.

This keeps the ground moist and prevents mulch from burying the seeds too deeply. After they have sprouted, I remove the box but leave it close by, and if frost threatens, it takes only a few minutes to go along the row and cover the tiny plants by turning the box over them. If there were a severe frost this might not answer, but so far it has done the trick. Then of course I thin them down to one plant.

I have also changed my method of growing verbenas; I don't try to start them myself any more, having persuaded Mr. Mead, the man from whom I buy pepper and tomato plants, to start them in his hot house. I love verbenas and this way I can be sure of having some.

Mr. Mead has started lobelias for me for several seasons, and at last I have thought up something to do with them which is effective. Up to now I've planted this charming little blue flower here and there as borders for flower beds; some of these are in part shade, some in full sun. The lobelia behaves differently in different spots; I'm not sure about this, but I think it usually does best in part shade. Mr. Mead always gives me many more plants than I can use, and one summer, because of a very early unprecedented drought, I left a flat of lobelias sitting near a tree and didn't get it planted; I kept it watered, and it was a welcome and bright spot of blue all summer when nothing else was behaving normally.

Now, in a row along the driveway are the three holly trees I mentioned, and here also were most of the hybrid tea-roses, which were the first things visitors saw when they drove in. I needn't tell you how unfortunate it has been for one who presumes to write and talk about how to garden to have callers greeted by those very unenthusiastic rosebushes.

This is a bad spot to try to make attractive, or even presentable, with flowers, for there's a good deal of shade and lots of tree roots around. Maybe you are thinking: no wonder the roses didn't like the location. Well, this occurred to me quite a while ago.

When Mr. Mead, this last spring, gave me the usual over-supply of lobelia plants, which were crowded into two or three flats, I transplanted them into other flats, putting the plants six or eight inches apart. The flats were then placed along the row of holly and I put mulch around them; the flowers look as if they were planted in the earth.

It is no trouble to keep the flats watered, when they need it, and of course the tree roots can't affect them, and the amount of shade they get seems just about right. What a relief it is (and what a change!) to have something bright and attractive to greet the eager beavers who drive in to look around.

When we plant a perennial we expect it to stay right there and live forever, or at least for a long time, and we're a little put out with it if it doesn't. But the things which seed themselves come, like a gift, each spring. Not exactly unexpected, but unearned and undeserved.

My mother called these little presents "volunteers." When, each season, the perennials began to show life—when lilacs budded, and bulbs and peonies pushed new growth up through the earth—she was of course delighted. But when new tiny seedlings peeped through by the hundreds (I really think it was thousands but I don't like to exaggerate) the pleasure in her eyes was mingled, it seemed to me, with surprise and even awe. Certainly with gratitude.

For years our place abounded with petunias; they not only seeded themselves year after year in their own spot, but began to show up around in other flower beds, and more than once a bright petunia or portulaca has made its appearance out in the vegetable garden.

Finally we ruthlessly pulled up most of the petunias, not because we don't like them a lot, but there's never room enough to grow every flower one wants; we decided to give some other things a turn. Undefeated, they continued to appear here and there in various beds, and we always let a few of them stay.

Then one year we had a very severe drought; this was before I had started the system of over-all year-round mulching for both flowers and vegetables, and that season we had no vegetables at all, and the annual flower beds were almost empty. We have a dug well and during a drought we can water nothing.

The reason our flower beds were only *almost* empty was because those amazing petunias, the few we had permitted to survive, kept right on blooming all summer, giving us the only spot of color on the entire place. Of course they looked small and thirsty and pathetic but they lived and blossomed.

Two summers ago we had another bad dry spell—no rain at all for sixteen weeks, but I was now mulching and we lost nothing. And one petunia plant, which I had allowed to remain in the bed of asters, thrived and spread and got so big and bloomed so generously that, in order to convince visitors that it was only one plant, I had to tell them to examine it.

Just outside the kitchen window we have a triangular bed of portulaca (I prefer its old-fashioned name: rose moss) which Mother planted twenty-seven years ago and it produces a countless number of new plants each year.

Since I now use a constant mulch over everything, I have to give the things which seed themselves a little special treatment. On some warm day in April or early May I pull back the mulch on these beds to the edge and give the little seeds a chance to sprout. When they are around an inch high I thin them with a tool which is almost like a scraper to six or eight inches apart (a foot apart might be better), then put a good-looking mulch around each plant. Another way to do it is just to put mulch on top of the plants you don't want.

For mulch for flower beds, where the appearance is important, I use almost completely rotted hay and leaves. My vegetable garden has an abundance of this which looks almost like dirt, yet is coarse enough to keep down weeds. It also holds in moisture and, this done, the rose moss bed blooms right through the driest summer. If you haven't mulched long enough to have a surplus of this kind of material, then peat moss, buckwheat hulls or sugar cane will do. But they are expensive; a less costly trick is to mulch with hay, leaves, sawdust, or weeds, then, for looks, cover this with a little dirt. However, rose moss spreads so quickly that even a rather offensive-looking mulch is soon covered up.

Rose moss also rears its pretty face in other flower beds; when I can, I leave it there, or give the plant to a friend; I guess there's nothing easier to transplant than rose moss. If you know someone who wants to start a bed of it, give him handfuls of your plants in the fall and tell him to lay them on the spot where he wants to make a bed of it; he will have one the following spring.

California poppies also seed themselves in huge quantities. I have these planted in my row of tulips and they are a mass of beautiful yellow blossoms all summer, taking the curse off the tulip tops that are unsightly when they are dying. As with anything which seeds itself, the mulch has to be pulled to the edge of the bed for a short time in early spring.

My intentions about thinning poppies are always good, and I announce each year that I am going to do it, but I never keep the promise. I have a young neighbor who hasn't grown flowers very long, and she still reads and believes garden books; one morning when she walked into our yard there was a bewildered look in her eyes.

"Your poppies are so gorgeous," she exclaimed, "a mass of yellow, and I don't understand it."

Although I had an idea of what was puzzling her I wanted her to tell me, so I asked: "What's the problem?"

"Well, I know that you don't thin them and there must be hundreds of them right up against each other but I just read an article which said that if you don't thin poppies to at least eight inches apart, you won't get any blossoms."

"When you read one thing, then see the direct opposite, I suppose you might better believe your eyes," I replied.

She agreed to that, but I went on to explain that possibly I could get away with not thinning them only because I had kept an all-year-round mulch on that bed for years; the ground consequently was extremely rich from rotting hay and leaves, was full of earthworms, weedless, and fairly moist through dry weather. Already a devout follower of my little-work method, she was easily convinced.

One hard lesson we gardeners have to learn is to be hardhearted; thinning is a painful process. Killing young live growing things is no fun. But sometimes you can at least use judgment; if, for instance, you are thinning a row of parsnips or turnips you can often choose the most promising one and pull all the others. And ruthless as this may seem, there's some reason and justification for your choice.

When, however, I thin a bed of rose moss, where the selection is usually arbitrary, where I have no reason at all for saving the one I may choose, I can almost hear all of the others reproaching me: "Why must *I* be the one to go?"

I have a new way of growing any annual flowers which I have trouble starting out of doors from seed. Last spring I filled small jiffy pots with a half-and-half mixture of rich garden dirt and vermiculite, with a thin layer of sphagnum moss on top, and put a few seeds of phlox drummondi in each. I thinned these to one plant and about the middle of May set the pots in the bed, eight inches apart. Somebody told me I was going to a lot of work, for a woman who holds forth about taking it easy, but actually it was less trouble than planting the seeds in the bed and thinning them—assuming that they came up and you had any to thin.

In fact, I'm so pleased with this performance that next spring I may branch out and start a few other things in the house. That may mean that the kitchen tables will be so full of plants that I can't cook—but what's bad about that?

10

Conservation is not enough

One afternoon in August I was expecting some visitors from New Jersey who had written to ask if they might come and see my gardening system first-hand, and when they turned into our driveway there was another car right behind them, an unexpected group, coming for the same thing.

After the man in the first car (we'll call him Mr. A.) had greeted me he immediately pulled out of his pocket a paper on which was written a lot of stuff in that secret code you get back when you have your soil analyzed; he asked me what this and that meant and I said I didn't know. I suggested that he have his local agricultural bureau interpret it. Then I spoke to the man in the other car (Mr. B. let's say) and his group, and we all went out to the garden.

There were the usual questions and comments. **Mr. A.** produced a little bottle full of bugs and asked me what they were; I didn't recognize them, but by this time I had discovered that Mr. B. was quite well-informed and we asked him about the bugs which he readily identified. From then on it was smooth sailing: Mr. A. was full of complicated questions and Mr. B. knew all the answers; I was tempted to excuse myself and go take a much-needed nap.

A few days later I got a letter from Mr. B. His name really does begin with B; he's a Mr. Beaumont, consultant of the Soil Conservation Service at Amherst, Mass. He formerly was State Conservationist of the Soil Conservation Service for Massachusetts. Just one more example of how smart it is of anyone not to pretend to know something he doesn't. What if I had held forth to Mr. Beaumont!

In his letter he said he was surprised that I didn't make a point of the importance of conservation when I wrote or talked about my method, and I replied that although I practiced it in a small way, I actually didn't know enough about conservation, in general, to be able to add anything to the subject. I told him that I was about to write another book about gardening and perhaps I would try to include conservation. He immediately sent me a little literature and generously offered to give me more information.

Although I at first intended to take advantage of his willingness to help, I've decided against just copying down and repeating what others have said about something which they presumably know a good deal about; at the very least they know more about it than I do. So it seems to me much more to the point to simply tell you that *Soil Conservation* is a monthly publication of the Soil Conservation Service, U. S. Dept. of Agriculture and that it is available directly from the Superintendent of Documents, Washington 25, D.C., for $1.50 a year.

It's true that my method of gardening is one way of conserving the soil. In an article by Mr. Beaumont in the February 1959 issue of *Soil Conservation* magazine, he says: "Mulching the soil with loose organic matter is one of the most effective conservation practices. Mulches not only reduce erosion to a minimum, they also conserve soil moisture, check weed growth, improve soil tilth, enhance the intake of water by the soil, and increase soil fertility when they decompose. They are particularly good in a garden because they prevent raindrop-splash erosion, which splashes soil onto vegetables."

J. A. Eliot, whom I mentioned in the chapter about asparagus, has two long columns in his latest leaflet about what he calls the Ruth Stout Mulch, tying it up with soil conservation, and saying in part: "In addition, this new system of plant growing gives promise of vital value to the nation. For it may become a big factor in saving the soil in the dustbowl. That bowl is a worse threat to the country than any foreign enemy because it is destroying one of our chief sources of food. For altho the Soil Bank Program is helping save some of the land, it isn't doing enough; on vast areas the soil is being blown like drifting snow. Do you know that

that's your land that's being ruined? For fundamentally that land belongs to us all; it's a part of the national bread supply, and no farmers or anybody have the right to destroy land, the source of all goodness. That land isn't adapted to modern wheat farming; instead it should be in grass, and the Ruth Stout mulch can help put it there.

"For when all horticulture discovers the value of this new system of plant growing, the demand for hay will become greater than the present sources can supply. As a result its price will rise to a point where, in the dustbowl, it will be a more profitable crop than wheat, and farmers there will grow it instead, thus saving the soil. Ask yourself if, for the sake of your children and the country, you don't want to help bring this about. If you do, help promote the Ruth Stout mulch. One good way to do this is to use it in your garden, and if you do, and do it right, you'll be rewarded with less work and better crops than you've ever had."

When people say that my system of gardening can never become universal because there just isn't enough mulch, I think not only of the leaves and rubbish that are burned every year but also of the many tons of garbage that go to waste. A few large cities are now collecting garbage and making compost of it, and many utility companies grind up the branches they cut from trees along the road; this makes an excellent mulch. A few years ago I talked to a garden club in Brookline, Mass.; these women told me that they have some arrangement with the town whereby all leaves are saved and made into compost.

And recently somebody in Hagerstown, Maryland, sent me a clipping from a daily paper there, saying that the city is now dumping all leaves on the fields of nearby farmers, that not one truck-load is wasted. We are learning a few things about conserving vegetable matter.

A New York City woman, who spends the weekends in her small place in the country, told me that when she buys supplies she asks the grocer to give her the leavings of vegetables which he throws away; her little boys are so fascinated with this project that they go all over the market in search of the produce which has the most waste on it, and insist that their mother buy only that kind. She has a successful garden, using only waste products. A tiny item, but there's nothing against multiplying it by several hundred thousand.

Americans as a whole are wasters in a big way, but I'm a natural-born conserver. And a fleeting joy, if it is *too* brief, makes me feel a little sad. For instance, a gardenia blossom, even one left on the bush, fades so quickly that I'm especially glad that it can be put back into the pot to nourish the soil.

There are other things which exist for a few minutes only, as far as any pleasurable or practical purpose is concerned, and I am thinking of gift packages. People put work into the production of tissue paper, others in making pretty boxes, and still others in manufacturing ribbon, then many people buy these materials and spend a lot of time wrapping gifts, and making fancy bows. But it takes only a few seconds to present the gift, and in a few more seconds the package is unwrapped and then what? Into the rubbish the trimmings go.

Maybe it's all worthwhile, though. I think most people, including myself, enjoy getting an attractive-looking package. I, in fact, like them so much that I have to use some will power to deliberately tear one to pieces. But at least I do it carefully and put the trimmings in the Good Will carton. I've never been able to make a pretty package and I don't try to do it; perhaps the reason for my awkwardness is unconsciously an unwillingness to spend time and money on something which will be given a fleeting glance and then destroyed, or maybe I'm just naturally clumsy.

I recently read how many acres of trees are used to make enough paper pulp for one edition of *The New York Times*, and the figure was so appalling that I immediately forgot it; I just couldn't stand it! Newspaper can be used for mulch or can be plowed under for organic matter, and we are told that the ink on it isn't harmful; if all of the old papers were used in this or some other useful way, those figures wouldn't have seemed so shocking to me. Also, if I were a newspaper addict I might not have minded much.

One day a young man came to our door and asked me to subscribe to some local paper, and I said, "No thanks."

. . . . *I recently read how many trees (or maybe it was acres of trees) are used to make enough paper pulp for one edition of the New York Times, and the figure was so appalling that I immediately forgot it: I just couldn't stand it!* . . . .

Then he asked me what paper I read and I said none, and he looked mildly astonished and asked how I got the news —radio? TV? I sort of hesitated, then muttered something about hearing people talk about what was going on, then

I said: "After all, if the President gets shot, or something, and I don't hear about it for a day or two, does it matter?"

By now the young man was so stunned that I thought to myself that I would just go on and tell him the whole truth and see if he would survive. I announced: "I've never read a newspaper in my life."

There was a full minute of awed silence, then he half-whispered: "What is it? A religion?"

Joseph Wood Krutch, in his *Voice of the Desert,* had a chapter called *Conservation is not Enough,* and I admire everything he writes, but since the saving of time, energy, soil, is my baby, it's perhaps little wonder that when I came to this chapter I thought: "Well, my friend and armchair conservationist, there isn't much that even you can tell me about that."

You guessed right, I was mistaken, and briefly I will try to pass on to you what I learned. Mr. Krutch doesn't go along with the assumption that the earth was invented with Man's pleasure and profit in mind; more than that, he warns Man that he is heading for disaster if he doesn't mend his ways. He tells of how ranchers made war against mountain lions and bobcats so successfully that the coyotes increased and became a menace. Then the government stepped in and poisoned the coyotes, with the result that ground squirrels and gophers took over.

One ranchers' association woke up and posted its land, opposing the killing of coyotes, weasels, hawks, and other predatory animals; they complained that government hunters and government poisons had almost done away with coyotes, that chain-killing poisons had about finished foxes and bobcats. This resulted in serious erosion because the rodents, thus protected, were killing plant growth.

Mr. Krutch says that to almost every animal, Man is the most terrifying sight of all and he quotes Albert Schweitzer, who says that we owe kindness even to insects, to make up for the necessary and unnecessary cruelties we have inflicted on nearly the whole of animate creation. Mr. Krutch thinks that few of us will understand, much less be guided by, such consideration, not being even dimly aware of any connection between conservation and a large morality. That few of us are likely to suppose that "conservation" might include something beyond looking after our own immediate welfare.

And then he tells us what has happened in the desert regions: cattle set to grazing, desert shrubs rooted up to make way for cotton and other crops, and these "watered by wells tapping underground pools of water which are demonstrably shrinking fast. . . . Soon dust bowls will be where was once a sparse but healthy desert, and man . . . will himself either abandon the country or die. There are places where the creosote bush is a more useful plant than cotton."

Mr. Krutch thinks that something should be done to stop these goings-on, and he asks if there is a missing link in the chain of education, law, and public works. He answers his own question: "And the thing which is missing is love, some feeling for, as well as some understanding of, the inclusive community of rocks and soils, plants and animals, of which we are a part. . . . Ours is not only 'one world' in the sense usually implied by that term. It is also 'one earth.' "

He points out that even knowing many facts doesn't seem to help us. People may know that over-use may render land useless, that the deer multiply when the mountain lions are killed off, and consequently new growth of shrubs and trees is eaten. They have heard of the marvelous insecticides, so effective that fish and birds have starved to death, how on one island insects had to be brought back to pollinate the crops, how you run great risks when you almost completely kill off a destructive pest, because you may starve out everything which preys upon it. Then the pest itself may return in a big way because its natural enemies have disappeared. Yet in spite of knowing all this, Man still hopes that an earth for his exclusive use can be created if he learns more and schemes still more shrewdly. He hopes he can someday beat the game; Mr. Krutch thinks that in the long run he can't; he believes that "the whole concept of exploitation is so false and so limited that in the end it will defeat itself."

Man, "the tyrant of the earth, the waster of its resources" and "from the standpoint of nature as a whole, a threat to every other living thing" has become also a threat to himself. His very intelligence may be his undoing.

There is no hope for keeping a balance in nature unless we realize that to some degree "the immediate interest of the human species may sometimes have to be disregarded," and that the good of the whole biological community conflicts with what is called the general good.

Toward the end of the chapter Mr. Krutch asks a question which he doesn't answer: "How can he (Man) come to accept, not sullenly but gladly, the necessity of sharing the earth?" He ends the chapter with a quotation from Pope:

> *Has God, thou fool! worked solely for thy good,*
> *Thy joy, thy pastime, thy attire, thy food?*
>
> *Know, Nature's children all divide her care;*
> *The fur that warms a monarch, warmed a bear.*

And then the comment: "This is precisely what most men even two centuries later do not really understand."

My first thought when I read those lines from Pope was: "Good heavens, were men already at it two hundred years ago?" Which was thoughtless; they have of course always been at it. And the more intelligence they use, the more skilled they become in the field of wholesale destruction of all kinds of animals, including each other.

I have read this particular chapter of Mr. Krutch's three or four times; it is a warning, it is saying to Man: "Watch out or you'll finish the whole caboodle of you." One might be excused if one's retort to that was: "Fine, go right ahead! Maybe we will get something more attractive if we start all over."

Those of us who haven't as capable a head on our shoulders as Mr. Krutch has, who aren't as good at thinking so deeply and so far, and who, even if we were, couldn't get it down on paper so expertly, can surely do some little thing toward preventing Man's downfall—if we decide we want to. Those of us who have a backyard can conserve things instead of wasting or burning them; we can, for instance, put our kitchen refuse on some growing thing instead of destroying the garbage. And in that connection I would like to tell this: Joe Krutch read my garden book, then wrote me from Arizona that because of the lack of water they didn't try to have a garden; later, I got a letter from him saying that he had been putting their food refuse in a certain area in his yard and after two months of this, he had found on that spot the first earthworms ever seen on that property.

When I talked to a group of women in Bethel, Connecticut in early November, the odor of burning leaves penetrated into the hall where they were holding the meeting; this seemed almost like a direct insult and was emphasized by the fact that everyone there, including me, was enjoying the smell. I would hesitate a long time before criticizing Nature, yet it seems to me that she slipped up in failing to put something—a touch of Limburger cheese, perhaps—into tree leaves. Did you ever smell Limburger when it happened to get hot?

I liked the Irish and redheads and to bring this one by all means.

They came and among other disparaging remarks the gardener made as he stood there looking at my fine row of carrots with extra large tops was: "You can't have carrots without plowing." Since some skeptics say that root crops grown my way will be crooked and twisted and I don't know what else, I pulled a couple of carrots to prove that these were large, smooth, well-shaped.

I said: "I had a carrot last year which served five people."

The redhead answered: "I bet they didn't like carrots."

I searched around in my mind and came up with: "My parsnips are always so big and so beautifully shaped that in spring when I talk at garden club meetings, I take one along to impress them. And it does."

The Irishman smiled tolerantly and asked: "What do garden club women know about parsnips?"

I kept on trying to convince him until his boss said: "Don't exert yourself. A year from now he'll be doing everything your way and pretending to everyone he thought it up himself. He may even think he did, by then."

This gardener was obviously an intelligent young man but it seems to me that intelligence has little to do with the ability to grasp immediately the advantages of some radical departure from the established way of doing things. There are two men in our neighborhood, both past middle age, both able and experienced gardeners, and as near as I can make out, of about equal intelligence. One of them told me and everyone else that my method was nonsense. Finally, after several years, he showed up one morning saying with a grin that he wanted to have another look before he started my method. He was at last sold on it because everyone around him was getting better results, with almost no work, than he did.

The other, Earl Dumas, is a tree man, but at one time he had had a commercial truck garden. He dropped in one day saying he had heard something about my having thought up an easy way of gardening. I took him to the vegetable patch, told him in just about two sentences all I didn't do and the little I did do.

He pulled back the mulch, felt the earth, stood up and said: "It makes sense. It will revolutionize truck gardening. I've been too busy to fool with vegetables but I'll certainly grow them next year—your way."

It is interesting and a little depressing to note that most of the individuals I've chosen to tell about here are either the bores, the difficult ones, or at best the die-hards. But that seems to be the sort of thing we want to tell about, to hear about. Who would bother to read newspapers if they were full of stories about people who are friendly to each other, rather than those who are at each other's throats?

A novel must be full of hardship of one kind or another, although there was a time when at least the skies cleared on the last page. But that ending has become too sissified. The story with a murder became popular, but that is now too tame; it takes at least three corpses to hold the interest of the jaded reader and a lot of beating up sprinkled generously through the pages, Guns, knives and nearly naked women on the cover aren't enough; the words "brutal" and "savage" are there in big letters to convince us that the book is worth reading.

I depore all this and yet how dull it would sound if I picked only the thoroughly desirable visitors to tell about! And I wouldn't know which ones to choose, for almost all of the fifteen hundred were easy to take. And I am probably wrong about the whole thing. It is good, surely, that our own lives aren't so full of beatings and rape and crime that it would only bore us to read about them; good that divorce and murder and major wars are still rare enough to make interesting reading.

I am sorry to say, however, that there is one bad aspect about my visitors which a large majority of them have in common: they don't take the trouble to let me know they are coming. Most of my friends, knowing this, jump to the conclusion that these people are inconsiderate, but I feel sure that it's merely a lack of imagination; they can't put themselves in another person's place.

Whenever I mention to them the chance they took of not finding me at home, they almost always answer that they would have tried again some other time, sometimes adding that they were out driving anyway, so it wouldn't have mattered. It doesn't occur to them that I might be busy at something which I preferred not to drop, might have guests, be eating, taking a nap, or even just disinclined to wander around in the garden. And that, since they had come, I would be unlikely to tell them that I couldn't escort them around and talk to them. Yet these very people always say that they hope it is convenient and that they don't want to disturb me and I think they mean that. Purely a lack of imagination.

This is, I suppose, partly due to the fact that I let it be known that everyone is welcome to come and they seem to think of me as an institution. After all, if you go sight-seeing to, let us say, some model school or factory you expect it to be ready and waiting for your inspection.

One woman, recently, practically said that. She and her crowd were from somewhere in New York State and when they said they had some trouble finding our place I snatched the opportunity to say:

"If you had let me know you were coming I would have given you directions. Besides, I might not have been at home."

This woman looked at me in surprise and asked: "Oh, aren't you always here?"

I felt like telling her that since I was a human being I did, once in a long time, have to go to the dentist and even went out socially on occasion, but with angelic forbearance I smiled and said: "Not always."

There was the family who came from some place over a hundred miles away who said they had been planning the trip for a year, had finally got a baby sitter for the children,

and here they were. They quite obviously couldn't afford
either the time or money to take such a trip to no avail and
I gasped; for once my concern was for them instead of myself:

"But what a chance you took! Why didn't you let me
know? I might not have been at home."

One of the women looked appalled at the thought and
exclaimed: "Oh, you just *had* to be!"

For her sake I was devoutly glad that I was. People have
made a special trip from as far away as Pennsylvania and
found me away. One man came from Wisconsin, just to see
my method, and didn't let me know until he got to New
York. He had to go back home at once and the only time
possible for him to come out was the next afternoon. I told
him to come, but unfortunately I was having guests and
therefore I wasn't able to give him the whole afternoon
as I would have liked to do.

He was an intelligent, appealing man, a commercial truck
gardener. I wanted so badly to give him all the help I
could. When I haven't anything else to marvel about, I
wonder why on earth he didn't write me before he set
forth.

For those who come and find nobody at home, Fred had a
sign painted which stands at the approach to the vegetable
patch and reads: "Fools Rush In—Be an Angel, Stay Out of
the Garden."

*. . . . For those who come and find nobody at home, Fred had a sign
painted which stands at the approach to the vegetable patch and reads:
Fools Rush In—Be An Angel, Stay Out!*

It is a feature in favor of my method of gardening that the soil can be walked on without packing it down. However, with my way of planting, little sprouts of corn, peas, beans may be growing under the mulch and not yet visible. Anyone, therefore, walking in the garden, might well be tramping on some little live plants.

I used to be surprised at the questions people ask, often because the answer seems so obvious and sometimes because it's such a trifle. If you wanted to draw a hasty conclusion you might decide that people are slow-witted, but I don't think that's it. I imagine that most people, if they themselves had thought up this way of gardening, would have gone right ahead, as I did, making some mistakes, yes, but easily and quickly finding the answers. Their difficulty comes from trying to follow another's directions, obeying rules instead of using their own common sense.

It took no special brains, I assure you, to think it up. That just happened. To stick to it after I started required belief in it, which I had.

During that first year a woman in Indiana wrote me and among other things asked: "Will it really work? I don't want to be laughed at."

I answered that, yes, it did work, but if she couldn't stand being laughed at, perhaps she'd better not try it. I was raised with eight brothers and sisters, four older, four younger, so I grew up being laughed at and thought it was a normal aspect of life.

I wish I could tell you about the gifts I have received from gardeners but there have been so many that I couldn't begin to include them all. The one that took Fred's fancy was a bottle of Canadian Club. A woman knocked on the door, said her name was Mabel Wilson and here was a little present and could she please see my garden? We weren't able to figure out the reason for the rather expensive gift until we got better acquainted with her and her husband, Grant, and found out that giving presents is their talent and pleasure.

The only gift I ever refused (or rather, I told the donor that if he left it I would give it away) was a bag of rock phosphate. He was surprised and said it would be beneficial. I answered that it probably would but I added:

"When I talk to people, particularly to garden clubs, you have no idea how effective it is to keep it simple. In describing my method I emphasize what you don't have to do rather than the few things you must do. Gardeners read an awful lot of stuff and most of it contradicts something else they've read. They can hardly believe me when I tell them *just* do this and nothing more. They don't grasp it; at garden clubs they keep asking what *else* I do, don't I put on this, feed the plants with that? I don't want to confuse them. If I used the rock phosphate I'd have to admit that, yes, I did put a bag of that on my garden and that would disrupt the stark simplicity of the whole business."

He left the phosphate anyway, but I didn't use it.

The several thousand letters I have received are like the presents, nice to get but impossible to tell about. I guess the ones I like best are those which pick some particular little incident in my book to mention, as when Irene Mason wrote that she was glad that somebody else liked to bite into an apple and hear it crackle as though it, too, was having a good time. Or when Mrs. F. B. Rosevear wrote that she burst out laughing when she read my reason for not learning to drive a car, which was that I didn't want to go anywhere. And it still is my reason, for that matter.

Other writers may get more interesting letters than I do but I'll match envelopes with anybody. Two I remember offhand are: "To Ruth Stout, the Mulch Garden Angel" and "For the Greenest Thumb in Connecticut," this one without my name on the envelope at all. That last one sounds impressive, something like "To the President of the United States," but when you know that we've had the same postman for over twenty years it doesn't add much to my glory.

People who are well enough acquainted with me to know

how I like routine, hate to be interrupted and dislike unexpected callers, are surprised that I don't mind (much) what
all of these goings-on have done to my privacy. I tell them
that if I had to go to a job from nine to five every day I
wouldn't expect any privacy. This is somewhat the same
thing only much better; in this project I have the good feeling that enough people are getting enough out of this thing
to keep me from minding that I'm at everybody's beck and
call.

But this doesn't mean, I hasten to add to my friends,
that they should all begin popping in without warning.

One day a car of mulchers drove in unexpectedly and
after we had visited the garden and they had come into the
house to put their names in the guest book one of them said:
"I know you say in your column that you wish people would
call up and let you know when they're coming, but after I
read your book I felt that we were old friends and I didn't
have to let you know."

Fred and I burst out laughing and he said: "Ruth has
her friends trained; they wouldn't dream of coming without first calling up."

I'm afraid that is close to the fact and I'm willing to admit that this may be an unlovely characteristic. But since we
all have shortcomings what's bad about being open and
above board about them? Well, about some of them.

Recently I heard that Amy Vanderbilt, the latest eti-
quette expert, says that, now that many women no longer
have servants, one shouldn't drop in on them without warning. In my ignorance I thought she meant that women
shouldn't be interrupted when they're busy doing their
housework, but it seems I'm wrong. I believe that she explains that a woman is now helpless, having no servant to
tell the invaders she isn't at home.

This aspect of it has never affected me either way; I
never did hire anyone to do my lying for me. When nothing
else will serve, I've always handled my own.

12

Be glad you're a food faddist

Said Adam to Eve
That serpent's naive
What he told me just now is a panic;
He said I'd be wiser
To use fertilizer,
The crops would be truly Titanic.
Says I: "Brother Snake
Go jump in the lake,
Here in Eden we garden organic."

That is Fred's contribution to the subject of organic gardening. Mine is almost as negligible, as far as writing or talking about it goes.

I was an organic gardener—if a somewhat unorthodox one—for several years before I ever heard the expression. Now I have been a practicing one for sixteen years, yet, when I decided to include a chapter here, telling what the term means, I felt inadequate. Then here came a letter from Dick, mentioning casually that he had just finished an article called "What is Organic Gardening?" I lost no time writing and asking him if he would please send me a carbon of it and let me study it. He did better than that; he told me

Here in Eden we garden organic.

that I was welcome to quote any or all of it, verbatim. So
here it is.

WHAT IS ORGANIC GARDENING
by
Richard V. Clemence

Organic gardening is not a new system of agriculture; it is nearly as old as mankind. Although in the
Garden of Eden there was no occasion to do more than
harvest the crops, you will remember that Cain subse-
quently became a "tiller of the soil," presumably enjoying organic techniques. At least, it is hard to imagine him opening a bag of ammonium nitrate, or
spraying potatoes with DDT. In any event, Cain's ca-
reer as a gardener was terminated, as a part of his punishment for slaying his brother Abel, so it is doubtful
if he merits honor as the founder of the organic system.

Organic gardening has ancient origins. But the use of
the term is comparatively recent. As commercial farming has moved further and further away from traditional practices, and as such developments as hydropon-
ics have proved workable, some term other than
"backward" has been wanted to describe gardeners
who follow older principles. Indeed, some other term
has really been needed, for organic gardeners are moving forward as rapidly as are the members of newer
schools of agriculture. They are merely progressing
from a different starting point and in another direction.

What is the starting point of organic gardening? On
what principle is it based? These are naturally rhetori-
cal questions, and I propose to answer them shortly.
First, though, let us try to clear up a few miscon-
ceptions.

To begin with, there is Sir Albert Howard and his
famous compost heaps. Sir Albert is widely regarded
as the father of organic gardening, and the compost heap as an emblem of a sort of fraternity of the

elect. All such notions are quite wrong. It is true that
Sir Albert was a great man, and that composting has
proved to be a fruitful application of the organic principle. But many organic gardeners now consider the
compost heap to be an outmoded device so far as their
gardens are concerned. Superior techniques have been
available to the average gardener for some time, and
except in special circumstances, the compost heap is no
longer in favor.

A second misconception is one continually repeated
in the garden pages of newspapers and non-gardening
periodicals. This is to the effect that organic gardeners
eschew the use of chemical fertilizers through ignorance of a fact lately discovered by the writers: namely,
that the nutrients finally reaching plants have the same
chemical composition whatever their origin. Actually,
this fact has always been taken for granted by organic
gardeners, and it is only very recently that soil scientists
have begun to raise doubts about it. Whether true or
false, however, the belief has no relevance whatever to
the question of preference for organic fertilizers, which
turns on considerations of a different nature.

There are plenty of other mistaken notions about organic gardening, but only one more need to be mentioned here. This is the idea that there is something
anti-social about the whole thing. Since organic methods require none of the ordinary chemical fertilizers,
and since the same methods control insect pests and diseases automatically and render poison dusts and sprays
superfluous, it is easy to imagine that organic gardeners
do less than their share toward creating income and em-
ployment for their fellow citizens. It is easy, that is, if
you know little about the subject. Organic gardeners
are actually the largest customers for a long list
of items for which the market would otherwise be small
indeed. Who buys most of the dehydrated manures,
bone meal, dried blood and other animal residues?

Where is virtually the only market for spoiled hay? How about sawdust, shavings, wood chips, peat moss, and so on? If you would rather eat eggs than cornflakes for breakfast, you may be unpopular with the makers of breakfast food, but the poultrymen will appreciate you. Of course, not all of us demand the same things. Why should we?

Now, to return to the questions, the basic principle of organic gardening is very straightforward and simple: It is to let natural processes do the work. Study these processes; try to understand them; and try to help them produce results. Otherwise, do nothing. In particular, do nothing that is in conflict with the basic principle. That is where the question of using inorganic chemicals, poison dusts and sprays, and so on, comes in. Such practices are inconsistent with the principle on which the system is founded, and hence must be shown to be advantageous on their own merits if they are to be admitted to the scheme. It is this matter of principle on which so many beginners go wrong, and on which so much misunderstanding exists even among experienced gardeners.

The beginner, having grasped the fundamental concept, is prone to make a fetish of it. To him organic gardening is Nature's Way, and is to be valued accordingly. Gardening practices take on a moral flavor, and right and wrong methods mean good and evil ones to him. Such results as he may get are hardly more than by-products of a righteous life, and he regards the poorest organic garden as preferable to any other kind.

More experienced gardeners, being already accustomed to judging methods by their results, are not likely to get unduly worked up over questions of principle. To the extent that they adopt an organic practice, they usually do so because they perceive an advantage in some specific feature, like mulching. For the rest, they tend to use techniques patterned after commercial farming, and to be satisfied with comparable returns.

What both beginners and experienced gardeners so often miss is the fact that the basic principle of organic gardening is derived, not from philosophical speculation, but from practical garden experience. If you can recall what gardening was like almost everywhere some forty years ago, you will see how true this is. All gardening then was organic though no one called it that, for there were no other kinds. Fertilizer then was chiefly manure supplemented by the animal derivations sold by meat packers and rendering companies. All these organic substances were cheap, and were applied to gardens with a lavish hand. What sort of results were obtained? Naturally, few reliable records were kept, but to anyone old enough to remember the typical home vegetable garden of that time, two impressions are strong. First, the yields were heavy, and small gardens used to supply large families with an abundance of food to eat fresh and to store. Second, and more remarkable, insect pests and diseases were virtually unknown in those gardens. The poison dusts and sprays so popular today had not yet been invented; and if they had been needed, no garden would have produced anything.

Have you ever thought what happened to this Utopian scheme of gardening? If you are too young to recall it, you may wonder if I am not merely dreaming over the fond memories of youth. I will say something about these a little later. Meanwhile, let us consider some established facts. Forty years ago there were more than twenty million horses on American farms, and in our towns and cities there were at least forty million more. In addition to the great volume of organic fertilizers yielded annually by the carcasses of dead horses, the living animals produced manure enough to cover more than thirty million acres of land. With all this fertilizer so plentiful and so cheap, other less plentiful animal fertilizers were almost equally cheap, for few gardeners cared much which kind they used. Chemical fertilizers were purchased hardly at all. The early companies knew well enough how to make them, but they had hard work selling them in the face of such competition.

It was the automobile that undermined this traditional organic gardening. As this machine displaced the horse except on farms, and as the tractor took over there, chemical fertilizers began to have potentialities, and their manufacture and sale became big business. At the same time, insect pests and plant diseases made their appearance as serious threats to commercial agriculture, and chemical dusts and sprays were devised to combat them. Since then, the growing of fruits and vegetables at a profit has increasingly become a scientific endeavor. The farmer with superior education and training who keeps in close touch with his experiment station and other sources of information can make money. Few others can, except by good luck.

If you have lived through these changes, you have doubtless drawn some inferences from them already. If not, you might like to now. To an innocent bystander, it looks very much as if the procedures followed by commercial farmers have been largely forced upon them by circumstances beyond their control. The question thus arises as to what gardening might be like for people outside this sphere of influence, if they made the most of their opportunities. Instead of aping the techniques of commercial gardeners, and trying to improve on their results in our spare time, why not go back to the gardening methods of our youth and see what can be done with them? Were the big yields and the absence of pests and diseases episodes of a past history to which we cannot return? Or were they logical consequences of practices that may be repeated at any time? There is an easy enough way to find out. The wonder is that so few have thought to try it and see.

I will admit that the results of my first efforts gave me pause. I had decided that the only reasonably fair trial would mean an all-out attempt to plant the sort of garden that Father used to have, and pretending that nothing had been learned since his day, use no sprays or dusts and no chemical fertilizers, and sit tight until the outcome was known. Frankly, I expected nothing much. I had followed up-to-date methods for some years, and had done better than most of my neighbors. I was therefore astonished to find that my yields had substantially increased, and that diseases and pests had not been serious at all. I could see signs of them, and was tempted to spray and dust, but found that small damage was done in the end. Here was food for thought, and it provided enough for many hours before the following spring. Like any experienced gardener, I realized that no two seasons are alike, and that procedures that seem to work well one year may never do so again. On the other hand, as I began to think about the traditional methods I had used, and how they differed from conventional practices, I began to see some possibilities. From what I knew about soil, I thought that the heavy application of manure to it might encourage the development of organisms that would feed plants and protect them against serious injury from insects and diseases. If so, a year or two of the same kind of gardening would pay large dividends, and I decided to continue. I tried to recall the various practices I had once known about that would be consistent with the idea of feeding the soil and letting the soil do the rest, and I applied these as I remembered them. I also thought of new ones. I kept records as I went and could give my results in detail. But all that counts is the fact that I shortly became an "organic gardener," just by returning to traditional techniques and trying to improve on them.

Before long I discovered that there was a growing literature on the subject of organic gardening, and that the revival and development of the older agriculture was engaging the efforts of an increasing number of thoughtful gardeners. J. I. Rodale was employing a more theoretical approach than mine and Ruth Stout a more practical one. But all of us, and many others, were pursuing the organic principle, not as an obsession, but as a way of gardening that gets superior results without special knowledge or effort.

The case for the organic principle rests, not on appeals to emotion, but on the returns it yields wherever it is intelligently applied. With no occasion for spraying or dusting, I regularly grow vegetables of the highest quality on an area of about five thousand square feet. The yields are at least as large as the ones I remember from my youth, and I am sure I recall these with reasonable accuracy. Improvements on the old techniques consist mainly of economies of space and labor. My crops are very closely packed and the returns per square foot are far above the average. Apart from the actual harvesting, I spend an average of less than three minutes a day on the whole garden throughout the season.

Now, I am not criticizing commercial farmers for the practices they pursue. I can hardly see what alternative many of them can have. For the home gardener, however, the picture is very different. My notion of gardening with nature is that I should put the seeds where I want the crops, and that nature should do everything else. Beyond planting and a little thinning and mulching, I therefore do no work whatever. If anyone else is getting better returns with less effort by some other method of gardening, I should like to hear from him. If you are not, you might care to give some thought to the organic principle, and to how you can best apply it to your own situation.

In reading this article my sister and I independently questioned the statement: "Since organic methods . . . control insect pests and diseases automatically and render poison dusts and sprays superfluous. . . ." So I wrote Dick that I thought this was a little strong, and that it might raise some doubts, since in my chapter about pests I say that I do have a few now and then, such as squash borers and cabbage worms. I added that although what he said was virtually true, to the careless reader or to the one who expected never again to see one bug after he had begun gardening organically, I was afraid it would sound exaggerated.

However, what with the profound respect I have for the way Dick's mind works, my letter was diffident, apologetic, just short of servile, and he replied:

"Dear Ruth:

"I am happy to note that your critical remarks are made in the proper spirit, though I have reason to doubt that such humility is as firmly grounded as it might be. It is a little late in the day for you to be making a show of respect for authority, and I am not being deceived by such nonsense.

"To begin with, I am very nearly convinced that organic techniques, in the larger sense of employing and aiding natural processes, *are* potentially capable of reducing insect pests and diseases close to the vanishing point. If a small fraction of the effort spent in developing more powerful poisons were devoted to this purpose, I think that results could soon be had. Only this summer, for instance, I had an experience that was brand new to me, and that has tended to confirm my beliefs.

"While Ellie was getting supper, I usually went out and wandered around the gardens, and occasionally wound up on cool evenings sitting on a warm bale of hay at the west end of the house with my back against the warm chimney. Among the attractive displays before me were twenty-five-foot rows of cabbages, Brussels sprouts, cauliflower, and broccoli, and busy with these were more cabbage butterflies than I have ever seen. At least a half dozen were on hand every evening, and earlier in the day there were always a few around. Since there were so many more than usual, I took it for granted that these crops were in for trouble, and I kept examining the plants for caterpillars. On close inspection I would find small holes in the outer leaves, and the green castings of the little workmen. But I found only two worms, both on one cabbage plant, for all my pains. Obviously, they had been there. But before doing any damage, they had vanished. Guess where they went? I never dreamed of such a thing.

"I finally got the answer one evening when, seated on my bale of hay, I was thinking for the tenth time that the wasps were getting altogether too thick again, and that I must get rid of them. With my attention thus focused on the wasps, I immediately saw something that had entirely escaped my notice before. Wasps by the dozen were working up and down my plants, scrutinizing them for tiny cabbage worms, and eating every one they could find. I watched this performance, then, long enough to feel reasonably sure about what was going on, and returned every clear evening thereafter in order to leave no room for doubts. The cabbage butterflies were doing their best, all right, but the wasps were taking care of the worms as fast as they hatched out. When I think about getting natural processes to do the work for you it is this sort of thing, as well as others more familiar, that I have in mind. I suspect that organic gardening is just beginning to scratch the surface, and that great discoveries remain to be made.

"Now, so far as the article is concerned, I deliberately made the statement in question seem a little strong without (I hoped) proving on careful reading to be untrue. For your book I am entirely agreeable to your editing the thing any way you wish, to make it fit better with the rest. It would certainly be safe to add an explanatory note of your own to any remarks of mine that look doubtful to you verbatim."

Well, I didn't change a word of his article, of course. But one thing in it surprised me—I didn't realize that compost heaps were going out of style. If that's the case I can stop wearing myself out, deploring that people use up so much time and energy fooling around with them, when all they need do is make their compost there on the garden where it belongs.

Next, I'll introduce a member of the opposition. Meet Dr. Arthur J. Pratt, specialist in vegetable crops at Cornell University and the author of *Gardening Made Easy*. He first saw my garden in August, 1956, just one year after both his and my books had come out. Already an advocate of mulching to some extent, he was curious about a garden which hadn't been dug up or cultivated for so many years. After looking the situation over, his chief comment was that I might have better results if I used chemical fertilizer instead of cotton seed meal. He also thought my crops would be improved if I dosed them with poison and he suggested that we make a test together in my garden. My part was to be the two ends of the patch and his the one-third running across the middle. I roped my sections off and broadcast cotton seed meal over them in late November at the rate of five pounds to every hundred square feet, taking pains not to let one grain of meal fall into the province of the opposition.

The following April Dr. Pratt showed up with a bag of ten-twenty-ten which he scattered over his section. He had intended to use ammonium nitrate but he said someone made off with his supply of that.

He also brought some cabbage, broccoli, and tomato plants that day. The seeds which we had chosen together had arrived some time before and I had planted some of them and they were up. I was careful to see that the same vegetables were put in the two opposing parts of the garden.

And he brought some poison containing methoxychlor,

malathion and captan, which he asked me to spray on his section every week until about two weeks before the produce was ready to eat. That was the only part of the experiment I disliked but I tried to stick to the agreement and the few times I didn't spray I had excellent reasons.

In July Dr. Pratt came to Redding again to look the situation over. Ed Lang had taken some pictures from time to time; there was no contrast worth noting in the opposing parts, just a few minor differences. Dr. Pratt's peas were a little bigger than mine, my peppers and parsley were in the lead. My cabbage had some insect bitten leaves, while his didn't.

We had had a frost on June tenth which had taken much of the garden, even some kohlrabi and early cabbage; I had saved the tomatoes by covering them with hay, but they were of course crippled and retarded. Also, we had had no rain since early April except for two brief thunder showers.

"My part would show up better if we had had some good rains," Dr. Pratt said wistfully. "So would yours, of course," he added, "but I put on such a heavy dose of ten-twenty-ten—twice the recommended amount—that even without rain it started things."

I was too diffident to ask him what he meant by that, since all my things were started too. And I knew perfectly well that without either his fertilizer or my meal the rich soil from rotted mulch would have "started things."

Toward the end of summer I sent Dr. Pratt a report. I told him I had always believed "them" when they said the use of chemical fertilizers would give quicker results; however, the first cucumber and the first solid head of cabbage had been in my section. Dr. Pratt replied that one such event here and one there was meaningless, and I wrote back that I knew that, but didn't a mother always boast about it if her baby got a tooth before the neighbor's child did? And I couldn't resist adding that the race between the Blue Hubbard squash plants was definitely in my favor.

About the middle of October Dr. Pratt showed up again,

to find that we had had several frosts and that everything had been harvested. There was plenty of produce to show him, but no way of telling, now, from which part of the garden the various things had been picked, and no matter, because except for the peppers, there had been no appreciable difference. I did, however, ask him to please take my word for it that the largest squash had come from my hills.

There hadn't been one Mexican bean beetle, not one corn ear-worm nor borer, no aphis on the tomatoes, not a cut worm, not a squash borer in the whole garden. So why spray?

Now about the peppers. Although I had had to put out new plants after that heavy frost, I had begun to pick ripe peppers from my section late in August. But in spite of the fact that the plants in Dr. Pratt's part had some flowers on them, not one pepper began to form until it rained in August, and none of them had time to mature.

This puzzled me until I figured out that because we had had no rain all summer, the chemical fertilizer hadn't been washed down into the ground until August which was too late for it to be really effective, while the cotton seed meal which had been scattered over my part of the garden the previous November had been carried into the earth by winter rains and snows. But if you put chemical fertilizer on your garden in the fall it will have lost its value by spring, they tell us.

And so, even though you may not care a hoot about organic gardening, my conviction is that the gardener who doesn't want to bother to water his crop and can't be guaranteed rain in the spring and early summer, is better off to sow cotton seed meal in November rather than try to depend on chemical fertilizer. More than that, if he doesn't mulch, in a summer as dry as that one was he will have to water or lose his crops.

Dr. Pratt and I had decided to write an article about this —that is, I was going to write it, submit it to him for corrections and comments, and we were both going to sign it.

When I sent it to him he read it, filled in one or two things I wasn't sure of and returned it, saying he was too busy to write the article with me, as we had planned. This puzzled me a little (or do I mean puzzled?) since all he had to do was read it and call my attention to misstatements, if any, which he had already done.

Organic Gardening and Farming had been waiting eagerly for that article, and I completed it and sent it to them but they refused it. Again, I wasn't puzzled, but disappointed. *Natural Food and Farming* printed it.

What did this "test" prove? Nothing. What was it supposed to prove? Well, I never was quite clear as to why the interested parties were disappointed. Did Dr. Pratt think his part would produce appreciably better than mine, and that my section would be infested with bugs and maybe, with luck, my tomato plants would choose that year to be killed by blight although they never had been? Did the organic people—well, what *did* they want, better than what they got? What came out so badly that they didn't care to publish the results?

Here was a piece of ground which was rich from many years of rotting hay and leaves. Without benefit of either cotton seed meal or chemical fertilizer it would have produced some good vegetables. Both Dr. Pratt's crops and mine, therefore, had the advantage of this rich soil and whatever else we might have put on would not, I should think, have produced any striking results. I hadn't expected any. As for the poison spray, we knew in advance that poison kills cabbage worms, so we found out nothing new there.

So why did I want a test at all? For two reasons: one, it presented a splendid opportunity for publicity for my easy way of gardening. My book had been out less than a year, only two or three of the periodicals which subsist on the advertising of sprays and chemical fertilizers had so far published any articles of mine and a piece, with a vegetable expert from Cornell as co-author, would, I thought, give me a chance to spread the good news.

Two, letters were flowing in in a steady stream by then, from all over the country, from Canada and several foreign countries, and many of them were from anxious women whose husbands were definitely not going to pay any attention to a dizzy woman who had dreamed up some cockeyed notion, telling *them* how to garden. The wives put it more tactfully than that, but even then I had become an expert at reading between the lines. Now I could send word to these husbands that a real live scientist—a *man,* no less—from Cornell University was interested enough in my method to make the trip all the way from Ithaca a few times in one season to see what was going on.

Now, wasn't I afraid of the results? No; don't you see that I had nothing to lose, no matter how it came out? I wasn't, and never had been, trying to make a case for organic gardening. I was simply showing that one could grow things successfully with almost no work. If anyone was so devoted to chemical fertilizers and poison sprays that he simply had to use them whether he needed them or not, it still wouldn't affect the main point: gardening without labor. And if everything in Dr. Pratt's section had been bigger and earlier than in mine I still wouldn't have minded. (Well, not much). It is possible that chemical fertilizer, if mixed with the soil, hurries and boosts a crop (when it rains); but if it does and if anyone wants a bigger head of lettuce a few days earlier and is willing to pay the price, who am I to try to educate him?

I am not saying a word in this connection about depleted soils and the inferior vegetables such soils give us. The easy and successful part of it I can prove; the other I cannot, so I will leave that to those who know more about it than I do.

Dr. Clemence touches on the fact that exponents of organic gardening are inclined to make a fetish of it. That's true and, conversely, you can say that the opposition makes a fetish of being against it. Agricultural experts, college professors and so on, come now and again to see my method and they work hard at trying to get me to make claims in favor of organic gardening which are unfounded on fact. Two of them, I remember, were all set to pounce; it was their misfortune that, friendly and polite as they were, I was on to them immediately. After a few vain attempts, one asked me:

"If you saw some insect was going to destroy your entire bean crop and knew of a spray which would save it, would you use the spray?"

I felt I could tell by the hopeful gleam in his eye that he thought I would give a lecture on the evils of poison, probably claiming, in my zeal to prove my point, that the sprayed beans would without doubt be the end of me.

I wrinkled my nose distastefully and answered: "I don't like the smell of those darn sprays. And I'm spoiled; by my method I get all the vegetables we can eat with practically no work so I wouldn't bother to mess around with a spray just for a few beans."

The other one asked: "How would you go about mulching a hundred-acre corn field?"—a perfect trap, designed to make me hold forth about something I couldn't know anything about.

I replied: "There are millions of people all over the world who want and need a little vegetable garden. When I get all of them to mulching I'll look into the problem of big corn fields for you."

Even so, we parted good friends.

Any new and radical change which doesn't interfere with the people who are financially concerned, such as styles, goes along smoothly, but a change such as organic gardening or natural food activities which threatens the money interests, brings out some passionate opposition. Discussion deteriorates into heated arguments, names are called, and both sides make claims which they can't substantiate. It is one thing to feel sure that you are right, but another to pretend to prove it when you have no actual proof. We only hurt our cause when we do that. Some people who are **against** depleted soils, poisons, devitalized and otherwise harmful foods, also hurt their cause, it seems to me, by never being able to talk about much of anything else. The most fascinating subject in the world can become boring if harped on too constantly.

The other side, the ones in favor of poisoned and inferior and harmful foods rely largely on name calling; how they love to sling the words "food faddist" around! And the people who are in favor of eating healthful and natural food are annoyed at this, but I don't know why it should bother them; before long the malnourished opposition will go to their reward, poor things, and the food faddists will inherit the earth (such as it is) and there won't be a soul around to call them insulting names.

. . . . Wasps by the dozen were working up and down my plants, scrutinizing them for tiny cabbage worms, and eating every one they could find.

13

Fit for a gourmet

Near us live a man and wife whom I will call Peter and Arlene. Peter has such a highly developed palate that it's just a little short of awesome and if I hadn't been sure of his tolerance I would have been in a state, at first, when I invited them to dinner.

But it is difficult to remain awed by someone you live next door to; not only that, Arlene told me that sometimes they drink instant coffee and since we not only grind our coffee, but roast it, you can imagine what that did to his prestige. The next, and more severe shock, was the news that he sometimes ate, and apparently relished, roasting ears bought in market. And all of the other vegetables, too, for at that time they had no vegetable garden.

I suppose that a discriminating palate is in part an educated one. I, who can cheerfully drink the "wrong" wine with the "wrong" meat and eat combinations of food which gourmets shudder at, would rather skip corn on the cob unless it's been picked just before it's cooked. If I am served vegetables in a restaurant I leave them on my plate; my strong preference for them freshly picked comes from having eaten enough of them over a period of time long enough to educate even my indifferent palate.

One day I took some corn to a friend, Michael Rifkin, who had never tasted it just out of the patch. The following spring he and his wife came to dinner for the first time and I served asparagus.

"You spoiled all other corn for me last summer; now you've ruined store asparagus for me as well," he said reproachfully as he began on a third helping.

Apparently he meant it, for his wife said that he no longer liked corn from the grocer's. She went on to say that she was afraid to ask us to dinner because she wouldn't know what to do about vegetables. That startled me; I would hate to get a reputation for being fussy about what I eat. For one thing, I would be a headache to my hostess and for another, people might keep putting off inviting me and the time might come when I wouldn't have a hostess to be a headache to.

There are other vegetables besides corn which should be eaten soon after they are picked in order to have them at their best. This is true particularly of peas and asparagus. When I gather a few stalks of the latter to be served for lunch or dinner I usually eat my share as I pick it, feeling that it deteriorates a little on the way to the house. I'd like to see any gourmet top that one.

Peas lose their sweetness rapidly, I think. I never serve them raw but I eat some as I shell them.

I don't know whether parsley deteriorates, either in flavor or vitamins, after it's picked, but it loses its crisp, fresh quality more quickly than almost anything else does. We eat a great deal of it raw; I rarely bother to use it in cooking.

I don't mind having to go out just before mealtime to pick corn, asparagus or parsley for it takes only a few minutes, but I was sorry when I heard that it was desirable to give peas, also, this special treatment and I tried not to believe it. But I gave in after eating them both ways, and although I would a little rather not pick anything which takes up as much time as peas do after six P.M., when I feel that housewives and gardeners, as well as job holders, should be through for the day, I do it. And, as is true with a great many other activities, I usually find that thinking about it and minding it in advance is worse than the doing.

Now I can either shell them at the kitchen table, hunched over a little, perhaps hurrying, perhaps wishing I didn't have to do it, or I can take them into the living room, settle myself in a comfortable armchair with a cushion at my back, spread a newspaper over my lap and shell and sip a Daiquiri and think about something pleasant. And I eat some of the youngest, juiciest ones and naturally I prefer the latter procedure.

If the nutritionists and flavor addicts have announced that lettuce is better picked at the last minute I haven't heard about it, so I bring ours in sometime during the day, wash it, dry it thoroughly (this, I hear, is important) and put it into the refrigerator until dinner time. You can dry lettuce effectively by putting it into a piece of cheese cloth and swinging it rapidly overhead. When spinach is in season we combine it with the lettuce and we always put in plenty of dill. Milkweed when young is good in salad and a bit of mustard (the plant, I mean) and of course parsley. Oh yes, and the leaves of celery.

I never add tomatoes to a tossed salad. For my taste they

You can dry lettuce effectively by putting it into a piece of cheese cloth and swinging it rapidly overhead.

make it too watery and somehow it seems to me that mixed with green leafy things which quickly and thoroughly absorb the dressing, tomatoes are at a disadvantage. I prefer them just as God grows them (with a little help from me) with nothing added, not even salt, or else sliced in a generous amount of French dressing and tossed thoroughly in it about an hour or two before serving them. The dressing has time to give them plenty of flavor and there's enough liquid for you to eat with a spoon along with the tomatoes if you aren't too elegant for such behavior.

Now, how are we going to proceed with all the other vegetables which are out there in the patch? Must we harvest them as soon as they are edible or may we wait awhile? Let's take them alphabetically.

BEANS: Some people like to rob the cradle; others are content to let the beans reach maturity. If you wait too long they will usually get old and tough, yet I find that the broad varieties may be allowed to get old and will yet stay tender. If you let beans get ahead of you, you can allow them to stay on the vine even longer and use them shelled. However, I read the other day that they will stop producing if you don't keep them picked and I'm inclined to believe that. Last summer I wondered why some of mine had sort of seemed to lose interest and I wouldn't be surprised if that was the reason.

BEETS will wait for you indefinitely, up to the first hard frost, especially Long Season. I'm not so sure about the earlier kinds; I've never asked them to wait. Some people prefer the tiny young beets; a good economical way to use these is to put off the thinning job until the beets are about the size of a big marble, and then cook them, tops and all. Another thinning when they've reached golf ball dimensions, and from then on have a meal when it suits you.

BROCCOLI and purple and white cauliflower must be picked as soon as they mature if you want them at their best. Otherwise, broccoli and purple cauliflower will begin to flower, and white cauliflower will turn brown.

CABBAGE will be patient for quite awhile but eventually the head will burst; then, even if I'm not ready to use it, I take it in, wash and dry it, wrap it and put it in the refrigerator. I think it is better off there, crisp and cold, than in the garden.

CARROTS will stay sweet and tender in the patch all winter long if you cover them well with hay.

CAULIFLOWER: See broccoli.

COLLARDS may be cut over and over; other leaves keep on coming.

CORN: Try picking it quite young and eating it raw. When we first moved to the country there was some corn disease around and people were forbidden to transport corn from New York State into Connecticut. My mother didn't know this. A friend drove her up to see us; on the way they passed a road stand in New York State with corn for sale and Mother, afraid that ours wouldn't be ready to eat, bought some to bring along. As they were about to enter Connecticut a young man from the State Agricultural Department stopped them and asked if they had any corn; when they said they had, he told them that they couldn't take it into Connecticut.

Mother smiled indulgently and asked her friend to pull up at the side of the road; she husked the corn, they ate four ears and Mother persuaded the young man to try an ear. With apparent relish he ate all the rest of it.

CUCUMBERS: We like these best when they are about the size of Fred's middle finger. We wash them and eat them as one does an apple. But of course I let many of them grow full size.

DILL: We eat some of the green, fern-like part almost every day. We don't pull up the root; simply gather it as one would a bouquet.

KOHLRABI will get tough and woody if left too long.

LETTUCE may be picked at any time before it goes to seed. We prefer it, however, when it's young, so I plant it fairly often.

ONIONS: The younger you eat them, as scallions, the milder they are.

PARSLEY: Just lean over and grab a handful every time you're in the vicinity and eat it then and there. It wilts quickly; if you want to garnish something with it and prefer not to have to pick it the last minute, you can put it in a glass of water as you would flowers in a vase and set it in the refrigerator.

PARSNIPS are at their best in very early spring but their season then is short because once they thaw they begin to get soft. It is good to know a few people to whom you can give some.

PEAS: We covered them earlier in the chapter.

PEPPERS: I grow an early variety so that they will ripen before frost. We think they are sweeter after they have turned red and nutritionists say they are then fuller of vitamins.

PUMPKINS: I used to be confused by that old poem which says "When the frost is on the pumpkin," for that sounds as though one leaves them out in the open until after a heavy frost. But poets are allowed some leeway as regards practical matters; I always gather pumpkins just after they've turned color and before a heavy frost.

RADISHES: You know you must eat them before they turn hot and pithy, but be sure to try Champion. It's surprising how long these stay mild and tender.

RASPBERRIES: The trick is to get them before the birds do, yet at the same time give them a chance to get fully ripe. Then when they have ripened grab them before they fall off the bush of their own volition. Raspberries really keep you on your toes.

RHUBARB: In spite of those authorities who tell you to pick it for only six weeks, I have been able to gather it from early spring to frost ever since I've been giving mine leaves, hay and garbage.

SPINACH: Any time before it goes to seed.

SQUASH: Before the first hard frost.

STRAWBERRIES: These, as you know if you have ever grown them, are so superior when picked at their prime, that they seem to be no relation to those sold in a store. My guess is that a home-grown Fairfax, picked ripe and eaten while it is still warm, not only would claim, but believes sincerely, that it is not even a distant kin to a store product, particularly Premier.

TOMATOES: I like to let these ripen on the vine although I'm sure that if I picked one partly ripe and let it finish the job in some dark spot (not in the sun) I couldn't tell it from the vine-ripened fruit. I believe, too, that we may accept the theory that fruit and vegetables aren't benefited by having the sun shine directly on them before they're picked. It is supposed to be the plant which needs the sun, not the fruit itself.

TURNIPS: We like them raw as well as cooked. They almost always stay tender, however big they get. They are noticeably sweeter after they have been frozen, but, unlike parsnips, you can't permit them to stay out all winter and expect to enjoy them in March. They go soft and rot. If you let them freeze in the ground, then sort of chop them out, run cold water on them until you can handle them, and peel and cut them up while they are still partly frozen and cook them, you will find them at their best. I am, however, not willing to go through all that just to get the best out of a turnip, much as I like them.

That seems to take care of the harvesting and now how are we going to cook all these things with the aim to preserve as much of their flavor and nutritive value as we can? One way is to eat them raw. We don't eat beans, beets, collards or rhubarb raw but many people do. Neither do I fool around with a juicer. It's a little overpowering to think how many fresh, raw vegetables (all very good for you) you can manage to get down if you drink them. But can't you see the pitfall? If you have arrived at the point where you think it is important to consume that many vegetables, you are no doubt against eating them if they have been poisoned or aren't organically grown. And I'm sure you want them fresh.

This would usually mean that you must grow them yourself because it is next to impossible for most of us to buy organically grown vegetables. And when I think of the rows and rows of carrots, not to mention everything else, I would have to grow if we took to drinking them, I am against making them into juice. Even by my easy method, even just picking them and washing them, I don't see how I would have enough time or energy left to raise the glass and drink to my health. And I feel the same way about sprouting various vegetables.

I know that these are fighting words and will outrage anyone who is devoted to juicing and sprouting, so I hasten to add that under certain circumstances I might act differently. If I had children to feed or if the maintenance of Fred's and my health seemed to require such goings-on and I could think of nothing easier which would serve the purpose I would probably give in. I have no doubt that both vegetable juices and sprouts are beneficial, but other things are good for us, too, such as lying on a couch and reading a good book. One has to make a decision; as things are now with us, I'll choose a nap, if juicing interferes with resting.

We are told that if we aren't going to eat at once the vegetables we have just picked, we should wash and dry them, leave them whole and put them in the refrigerator. If we are going to cut them up this should be done just before they are cooked. They should never be left to lie in water at any time, should be cooked with as little water as possible, and if any liquid is left it should definitely go into somebody's stomach.

I have read that vegetables should be cooked rapidly and that they should be cooked slowly; take your choice. As to that, everything in the above paragraph is quoted from the authorities; since I am not a scientist I would be hard put to prove that any of it is correct. I follow it, because it sounds all right and at least it seems to me that none of it could be injurious. After all, we have to more or less trust somebody until we find out he is wrong.

What else are we told? That we should under-cook rather than over-cook all our food except, of course, pork. That leftovers are more nutritious if we don't warm them up.

This is easily got around by putting some French dressing or sour cream on leftover vegetables; Fred likes them better this way than hot.

By all means steam your corn, don't boil it. And if you cut it off the cob, try this: put about a tablespoonful of water on it, get it steaming hot, add as much butter and salt as your conscience will permit and serve at once. You actually don't cook it at all; just be sure it's hot, all through.

If you are against using salt and butter for seasoning, try a spoonful or two of Energy Broth. Many health food stores carry it. It has a delicious flavor and is made of raw, naturally-grown vegetables, nuts, seeds—well, get a can, make yourself a cup of broth and read the label telling you what's in it while you drink it and you'll fairly feel yourself getting young and healthy. The first time I used it to season a French dressing on a tossed salad everyone asked what on earth I had used to make it so delicious. There is one drawback: it's supposed to keep you in such good health that you'll live to be 160 years old. Who wants to live so long that he has no one to talk to but immature eighty-year-old youngsters?

I defy you to make green beans taste any better than by cooking them slowly for a couple of hours with lean bacon or ham, but don't do it; the nutritive value has fallen by the wayside.

Try mustard and sour cream on cold cooked carrots.

If your cucumbers do anything at all they are likely to go too far. You have too many in too short a time. You might try this: slice them paper thin, add raw honey and vinegar to your taste. Put them in a Mason jar (don't bother to sterilize it), be sure the liquid comes right to the top, seal the jar and serve in the winter. You needn't make a project of this; every few days pick what cucumbers are ready, fix them all, eat what you want now, and can the rest. If they get ahead of you and get large and ripe, peel and slice them, take out the seeds, cook them until tender in raw honey, vinegar and pickling spice. Put them in unsterilized jars. Everybody seems to like them; they make an acceptable little gift.

Years ago I read that one could cut up rhubarb, put it in unsterilized glass jars, cover with cold water, seal and store in the cellar for winter use. The advantage over cooking it is that you can have it raw, for pies, all winter long. A visitor to my garden this past summer mentioned this and said they always did it so I put up a few jars although it was then late in the season. I opened one of them in December; it had lost its red color but the flavor was intact. I cooked it with all the water I had covered it with, for I assumed that much of the value had gone into the liquid. So of course it was almost all juice; you could strain it and drink it if you wanted to or do as we did: put a big gob of cheese with it and eat it with a spoon.

I hope that nobody evades the job of freezing his vegetables because he thinks it's too much trouble. I find it so little work and so worth while!

Let's take asparagus as an example. As you know, it must be picked every day or it will get too old. You may be going out to dinner, or there may be enough for two or three meals ready to pick; you must gather it if you don't want to lose it.

The picking, if you snap it off where it's tender rather than cut it, is a matter of a few minutes. Back in the kitchen you turn on a burner and put on it a large pot with about two cups of water in it. Also, a collapsible steamer if you have one; if you haven't it isn't very important.

While the water comes to a boil you run cold water over the asparagus; this takes only a minute or two for it is neither dirty nor tough. The vegetable is put into the pot when the water is boiling hard and you turn the timer on to ring in five minutes.

Now you get out whatever containers you are going to use. I like to wrap the asparagus in polyethylene and put it into candy or cookie boxes. It doesn't matter what size they are, for I have found that frozen asparagus stalks are easily separated from each other. When I open a package which has too many for my present purpose I take out what I need and put the rest back.

When the timer rings I cool the asparagus under running cold water, then put the stalks in the boxes and store them in the freezer. I may easily have done enough for four meals, and the whole performance, including picking, has probably taken me less than fifteen minutes.

Broccoli and cauliflower are as quick and easy to freeze as asparagus. A head of cauliflower is often too large for one meal for our family; if I don't want to cook it all and use what's left for salad, or eat it raw, I freeze the surplus.

With the exception of peas and beans which take time both to pick and to prepare, most other garden products take only a little longer then asparagus.

Beets, contrary to the general notion about them, freeze perfectly; cook them until tender, cool gradually, then freeze them. What one sacrifices in vitamins by this method, I can't tell you, but one loses nothing in flavor.

I no longer freeze corn. The flavor remains but the crispness doesn't, so we eat it in season only.

You can grind up parsley and freeze it; I went a little off balance a few years ago and ground and froze a bushel and a half of it. This I don't advise.

I cook winter squash as though I was preparing it for the table, then freeze it. I like to combine a very dry and a more watery squash (or a pumpkin) which serves two purposes. Pumpkin or Butternut squash, if cooked alone, will come out slightly watery. Buttercup is so dry that unless you hang over it and baby it, it is necessary to use a slight amount of water when you cook it. So if you combine them, the pumpkin or Butternut will supply all the liquid you need for both.

Even so, you must watch it carefully at first and start it on low heat. When it's tender I mash it and put it in containers and freeze it.

Blue Hubbard isn't as watery as Butternut nor quite as dry as Buttercup which is fortunate, for they are so big that it would be a bit complicated to combine them with anything else. One winter I had one of them lying under the kitchen table until May. It was so big and handsome and attracted so much admiration that I kept putting off cutting it up. Besides, I had plenty of smaller ones. I finally cooked it and we ate squash all summer. Even when the garden is full of fresh vegetables it's pleasant to have one in the freezer which requires no work beyond heating it.

Few people eat pumpkin as a vegetable and I wonder why; everyone seems to like it when I serve it. I season both it and squash with a small amount of salt, a little brown sugar, some grated nutmeg, and either butter or cream or both. We like sour cream in it as much as the sweet. If you like pumpkin (or squash) pie and are not in the mood to make the crust, bake the filling in custard cups.

I don't know how the word got around that you can't freeze tomatoes. It's true that freezing softens them and you can't take them out and slice them and use them in salad unless you are willing to eat them while they are still partly frozen as some people do. Since I can get along without them with tossed greens even when they are fresh out of the garden, I naturally don't go for using them when they are still frozen.

People go to the trouble of canning tomatoes in order to have them for stewing or soups or sauces, yet it seems to have occurred to practically no one that they can freeze them instead and use them for those purposes. You can cut them up without peeling them and put them in a container raw and freeze them. If you have enough space in your freezer you can have tomatoes all winter long which taste as if you had just brought them in from the patch. If you like, you can put them quickly through a sieve and drink them. Sometimes I eat them with a spoon, just as they are, cold, raw, and tasting like a fresh tomato. Some I make into juice (raw) when I bring them in from the garden, and freeze that.

I don't believe I ever live through a whole day without

asking myself at least once: Why? Why did he do this? Why do people do that? I seldom find the answer. Here is a question that keeps repeating itself: Why do people eat tomatoes and strawberries from the grocer's in winter? I don't think I feel superior to these people; I hope I don't, for I rather pride myself on not feeling above or below anybody. But I am a long way from understanding the reason back of this performance and I'm not sure that I want to. I have a notion that if I did it would depress me.

Now here are a few quick, easy and (we think) delicious recipes. Let's say you have carelessly invited someone to lunch on a very busy day. You have asparagus in the garden, and who doesn't like that, but what to serve with it? Cold cuts would look as though you had given the matter no thought at all, and deviled eggs take time which is just what you haven't got this morning. The answer, then, is:

ASPARAGUS WITH SCRAMBLED EGGS

Cut the asparagus in inch-length pieces, and cook the bottom-ends first in a large frying pan in very little water. When nearly tender, add the tips. After the guest arrives break some eggs into the pan, add a dash of cream and seasoning to taste. Dehydrated onion helps. Scramble, serve the dish as though you were proud of it and the luncheon will be a success.

But maybe the asparagus season is over, or perhaps you have no eggs on hand. Well, here is something else just as simple and even more tasty.

CHEESE WITH THIS AND THAT

Almost any vegetables will do (except perhaps carrots, beets, or parsnips), either left-over ones or freshly cooked. Edible pod peas are especially good. Cut Cheddar cheese into fairly large chunks and put it into the pot with the cooked vegetables. If you happen to have a cooked potato or two or left-over rice, or both, add them; they not only increase the quantity but also the quality.

You can either just heat this until the cheese melts, and serve it, or put it into a casserole dish, sprinkle some prepared stuffing on the top and heat it in the oven. If you have added potato and rice you will need to moisten the mixture with a *little* milk.

While I was preparing this dish the other evening for our dinner, a neighbor who dropped in for a minute was so taken with the whiffs he got of it that he hounded his wife until she made it.

But let's say it's a hot day—or perhaps your expected guests are raw food addicts. Give them this:

RAW CARROTS WITH RAISINS

Wash some carrots, then cut them up rather fine, add a liberal supply of raisins, then mix in some mayonnaise or sour cream. You may want to add some seasoning.

Good appetite!

14
How's that again, Professor?

If a person hasn't got what it takes to open the window of his car, it's a help to be able to do it by pushing a button. The snag is that the handy contrivance may get out of order and then he may be worse off than if he had learned to do it by himself.

In a sense, scientists are like gadgets—sometimes they are dependable, sometimes they aren't. But at least we know when a gadget isn't working properly, while with a scientist we often can't tell until, perhaps, it's too late. So when can we believe them, trust them, follow their advice? Well, we can, of course, if what they say coincides with our own experience. And here is a case in point:

A few years ago I read an article called "How I Got Free Mulch" in an issue of *Organic Gardening and Farming.* I found it interesting and valuable, but two sentences bothered me: "The matter (meaning the mulch) should not be put down while still green during the growing season, for it will rob the plants of nitrogen during its decomposition. This is a cautionary note that should be observed carefully."

I wrote to the author, Archer Martin, told him that I had put green (unrotted) matter on everything for thirteen years and had never had reason to think I shouldn't have, even during those years before I had used cotton seed meal to supply nitrogen. I asked him how he knew it was an unwise thing to do.

He wrote (saying that I might quote him) ". . . nitrogen is needed for the decomposition to take place, just as it is needed for the process of growing. Seemingly, the decomposition process is stronger than the growing process, for I've heard all my life that nitrogen for decomposition will be robbed from the plant trying to use it for growing."

Mr. Martin added that he was not a gardening expert and I felt that I had better look around for a more authoritative opinion. Before I got down to it I read in a later issue of the same magazine under Questions and Answers: ". . . you were right to apply cow manure—but the manure should have been well rotted. Fresh manures need nitrogen to aid the material to decompose, therefore the soil is deprived of the nitrogen content until the manures have decomposed and only then does the growing plant receive the nitrogen."

I hadn't used manure for ten years because under my method my soil was so rich that I no longer needed it, but when I used to use it I always preferred it fresh and found it satisfactory, so this note, too, was contrary to my experience.

I wrote, then, to two scientists, one of them connected with a large commercial seed house, the other, Professor Pratt, of Cornell University. Dr. Pratt sent me Cornell Extension Bulletin No. 886. Since the letter from the seed house and the bulletin and Dr. Pratt's letter all said exactly the same thing in different words, I will quote only the letter, which Dr. Pratt gave me permission to use.

He wrote: "Yes, leaves, hay, straw, etc., that are not decayed or that are only partially decayed will rob the soil of nitrogen if they are mixed into the soil. But when used on top the way you use them, I have never seen a nitrogen shortage as a result of the mulch. Of course, if there was not enough nitrogen in the soil in the first place the mulch materials do not add any for at least a long time, so they would not help a shortage nor add to it.

"I have never seen fresh manure, even when mixed with the soil, cause a nitrogen shortage. If it did it would be because of a large amount of straw mixed with it and the shortage would be very temporary. You could even get a temporary shortage from using cottonseed meal early in the season when the ground was cold and wet. The reason for it is, of course, that bacteria first have to break down the rather complicated organic compounds to make them available to the plant in the nitrate form. In doing that, the bacteria use the readily available nitrogen for their own growth. In a few days to a few weeks they die and release that nitrogen to the crop."

These scientists merely confirmed what I already believed, from my own experience. And I wouldn't have taken the trouble to find out what they thought in this instance, since I was doing all right without them, if people from all over the country hadn't been, by that time, writing and asking me every possible question they could think up about gardening. Now, when they asked me about this nitrogen-robbing performance, I could add the opinion of the authorities to my own puny experience.

Shortly after my first garden book came out, four professors of agriculture from the University of Connecticut drove into our yard. The University had tested my soil eight months previously (after twelve years of my labor-saving method) and had found it "well supplied with all major plant nutrients . . . and the ph value just about perfect."

One professor after another piled out of the car, every one of them young, pleasant, attractive, and even friendly. We went to the vegetable garden; I like to think that they were impressed with my soil, black and rich from years of rotting mulch, but unfortunately not one of them was the gushing type. They pulled back the mulch and there was the evidence, my allies the earthworms, right on the job, and one professor said:

"Well, well! The other day I looked for half an hour and found only one earthworm to fish with."

Two of them began to whisper over the corn and I begged them not to be so secretive, so they told me that the striped leaves meant that there wasn't enough magnesia in the lime I was using.

There were no weeds in the garden except some milk-weed in the asparagus and I told them that I purposely left that because we liked it in salad. They said the roots went all the way down to China and that I might be sorry. The next morning out came the milkweed, with regret.

There wasn't one bean beetle to be seen, and our visitors were surprised when I told them that I hadn't sprayed, and had planted the seed about the 20th of May. They said that if you waited until June to plant beans you were less likely to have bugs. Speaking of pests in general, one of them said that a healthy plant is safer from bugs than an unhealthy one; he said he had seen this to be true over and over in fields of alfalfa. (Poisoners please take note!)

They inspected the flower beds, me hoping I might get a little praise for making them presentable with my use of half-rotted mulch. But no comment. Then we went into the house and Fred served cocktails, hoping to loosen the professors up a little. But they were cautious, and I should be the last one to cry about that, since I am constantly going on about people who, writing and talking about gardening, carelessly make dogmatic claims and rules.

However, when I got up my courage and asked them outright what they thought of my method, three of them glanced at the fourth, who probably was the Big Shot, and he said: "For flower and vegetable gardens it seems to be an excellent idea."

That satisfied me.

A few weeks after that, Dr. Pratt (as I said earlier) came from Cornell. I told him that the Connecticut boys had said that my corn lacked magnesia, and he said he didn't think so, that it was nitrogen that it lacked. I had already given it some Dolomitic lime for magnesia shortage, and was willing now to give it nitrogen but I did ask this:

"If it is lacking in either or both, why should I care since I get two fine ears from almost every stalk and since it has never been more delicious than it has this cold summer, in weather which is supposed to be bad for corn?"

He grinned and answered: "You'd get bigger ears, maybe."

Here is a peculiar thing: while a professor is talking to me I feel humble, trusting him utterly, but just let him get out of my sight and I begin to think: "well, interesting, if true." By the time the University of Connecticut and Cornell scientists were all back home where they belonged I didn't feel at all sure that my corn lacked anything.

It is easy enough to see that when the scientists (whom I compared to gadgets) contradict each other they have lost their value for the layman. But let's not throw them on the trash heap prematurely; we may find *some* use for them.

I read a highly authoritative-sounding article called "Plowing IS Important" in the *Rural New Yorker*. The writer tells us why it is; he gives detailed explanations of how pinhead-sized pieces of soil cluster together to form aggregates, and how soil compacts, and how and why the water table is reduced, and all that sort of thing. He seemed to know what he was talking about, but does the average person with a vegetable patch give a darn about all this so-called knowledge if he is producing satisfactory crops without the work of plowing or spading? Can you imagine digging a carrot or beet or parsnip big enough to knock a scientist down with and at the same time worrying about "aggregates"?

I feel sure that the digging addict who wrote this article (I've forgotten his name) doesn't plow up his asparagus and rhubarb beds every year. I wish he had told us why the dirt under those crops doesn't form aggregates and get compacted and all the rest of it.

To go back to Dr. Pratt in this connection, when he visited us Fred asked him why people kept on plowing and he laughed and replied: "Just because they always have, I suppose."

Later he wrote me a letter in which he said: ". . . your long experience with no plowing and fitting should be helpful to all of us. If good yields can be maintained for ten or fifteen years without plowing or fitting, they probably can be maintained so forever on similar soils."

I didn't know what "fitting" meant but apparently it's a term used for harrowing and so on.

Now and then some expert announces that digging is necessary for aeration of the soil. Leonard Wickenden says in his large, impressive book on gardening: "I shall still feel that some disturbance of the top-soil is needed for aeration and that the judicious use of my fork and cultivator is the surest way to obtain it." But two scientists of the Ontario Agricultural College, Guelph, have found that there is more air in mulched soils than in non-mulched; in their words ". . . maximum respiratory activity occurred in mulched soils."

The gadget needs fixing again.

But in fairness I mustn't forget to say that one visiting professor told me that my gardenia needed iron, which turned out to be true. That's the trouble with experts; if they were always wrong we could forget about them and relax, but every now and then they hit the nail right on the head.

The profit in reading most garden books eludes me but I did get into one recently by a sort of accident. It seemed to me to be too long drawn out and too involved and "scientific" for the average gardener, for whom it apparently was written. As near as I can judge from the large number of people I have talked to in the past five years, and have had letters from, not many of them would be much interested in what happened in past centuries in the realm of gardening. How subsoil was formed, and so on.

This author (Leonard Wickenden, whom I mentioned above) did at least sound as if he knew what he was talking about until I came to his conclusions about mulching. He admits that he had never mulched his garden, yet he goes bravely ahead and explains what's "wrong" with the idea.

He says: "Weeds are by no means entirely eliminated," which is misleading, for he certainly gives the impression that he is talking about all, or at least most, weeds. The fact is that if you mulch deeply enough all weeds are eliminated except a few perennials, and I now believe that Dick Clemence has found that they, too, can be dealt with through proper mulching.

Next, Mr. Wickenden states that if a garden is mulched, light rains will do it little or no good because the moisture will be spread out in a thin film over the hay and will evaporate. Since he doesn't mulch, he must be speaking from theory only, which reminds me that according to all the known laws of physics, bumblebees can't fly, yet they keep right at it.

And I go on mulching, while experts sit at their desks and figure out that my garden is at a disadvantage as far as light rains and drought are concerned. As Benjamin Stolberg puts it: "An expert is a person who avoids the small errors as he sweeps on to the grand fallacy."

Well, here are some facts: since I have no water to spare for plants during a dry spell, I had more than one crop failure during fourteen years of plowing and cultivating. But for the last sixteen years, during which my plot has been covered with a constant year-round mulch, I have *always* had successful crops, even though several of those seasons were exceedingly dry; one summer we had a four-month almost complete drought, and that was the year my produce included a fifty-one pound Blue Hubbard squash. The bumblebees and I are doing all right, in spite of the scientists.

Mr. Wickenden also declares that the ground needs the direct sun in the spring to warm it up, but I have found this to be true only of the sections where the earliest crops are to be planted. And since you have to pull the mulch aside anyway, in order to plant, it isn't extra work to push it back ahead of time and let the sun reach the soil. Of course you have to be blessed with a mind which can figure that out; I submitted the problem to my niece's daughter, eight-year-old Jan, and it took her only about a minute to come up with the answer.

In an issue of the *Rural New Yorker* Dr. Pratt writes about mulch and even if he had got a little off the truth as I know it from experience, I would probably ignore it. But he has things to say about "a" garden which is obviously mine although he doesn't say so, which are misleading. He says that "this garden" often freezes in June and he then states flatly that this is because it is mulched. Now I'm sure he believes that, but it doesn't happen to be true; I lost my plants over and over through the years before I mulched. The unfortunate fact is that my garden happens to be in a frost pocket, and my plants, mulched or unmulched, often freeze when those of my neighbors' don't. The vegetable garden directly across the road from mine, not one hundred yards away, which is also heavily mulched, often doesn't freeze when mine does. I realize I've said this before, but apparently I can't say it often enough to get it into the heads of the experts.

Dr. Pratt is mistaken but even if he were right, I think it's too bad for him to discourage people from trying out my method of easy gardening. In a mulched garden, with the hay so handy, one can quickly, easily, toss it on corn, tomatoes, peppers, beans, when frost threatens. My plants no longer are killed by June frosts as they were when they weren't mulched, because it's so easy to save them with all that hay so handy.

Dr. Pratt does his utmost to make the situation sound grim. He warns: don't mulch until danger of frost is past, unless you want to stay up all night and irrigate.

Tut, tut, Professor! Toss a little hay on the tender plants

and go to bed; it's as simple as that.

Somebody told me that if you mulch you must use fine chopped hay that's free of weed seeds. The hay I use reeks with seeds but with an eight-inch mulch they can't sprout. This man also said that it's almost impossible to handle long coarse hay. One word will cover my opinion (resulting from handling long coarse hay) of that remark: Nonsense!

Why does it distress me to have the Big Shots talk against year-round mulch? Because scores of people have told me that they wouldn't be able to have a garden at all, for one reason or another, if they hadn't learned of my method. If any of the things which have been written and said against mulching has dissuaded even one woman with arthritis, or an old man, or an overworked mother with small children, or one victim of heart disease, or one commuter, from trying out my system, I am sorry indeed. I should think experts would think twice before condemning something which others have found to work successfully.

Of course laymen too, including me, draw hasty and incorrect conclusions. I even drew one in advance when I said in my first garden book that I had no way of spreading the news about my easy way of gardening, with all the garden magazines depending for survival on advertisements of sprays and chemical fertilizers automatically opposed to my message.

I was wrong. I know of no garden magazine or farm paper which hasn't carried one or more articles about my method, written either by me or some other enthusiast.

But it took some time and a little doing. *Popular Gardening* was the first to recognize its value to their readers. They carried a feature article about it; when I wrote to Mary O'Brien, then managing editor (she is now the editor), and expressed surprise that they wanted an article about gardening which said that sprays and chemical fertilizers were unnecessary, she answered: "Gardeners are becoming increasingly interested in organic gardening, and our aim is to help our readers in every way we can."

When this article came out someone wrote to a friend of mine saying: "What pleased me and certainly surprised me since *Popular Gardening* exists on advertising, is that they printed it . . . What I got the biggest kick out of was her statement that she plants and picks and that's all and her words all surrounded by the most alluring cultivators, hoes, etc., being advertised for sale. Maybe the world is slowly changing again and the manufacturers haven't got as tight a grip on us as we feared."

In my thoughts I am often catching myself drawing too-hasty conclusions; one example is enough as long as I admit there are many others. Two years ago I read that lilacs thrive if given woodashes. Ours were doing all right but I never had got firmly settled in my mind the question as to what was the best thing to do with the ashes from the fireplace. I had always found it a nuisance to sift them and yet I had to if I was going to put them any place where I might walk on them. Since I often burn wood which might have nails in it and since I go barefooted out of doors whenever the weather permits, sifting was necessary.

So, all winter long that year the unsifted ashes were dumped around the lilac bushes and in spring the "result" was most gratifying. And although I hold forth about drawing a conclusion from only one performance, I was all set to spread the glad tidings: woodashes do wonderful things for the lilacs. But luckily, before I got launched, I glanced around and saw that everyone had semi-sensational lilacs that season.

I said something about all this recently to a man who came to see my method and he answered: "That isn't surprising in an inexact thing such as gardening, with so many outside factors involved, but I think you would be surprised at how true it is in my work. I have been an accountant for forty years and I wish I knew how many contradictory conclusions I've run up against. Many more than you could believe, I'm sure."

There was a woman who read about my year-round

mulching, got enthusiastic, spread great quantities of hay over her wet, clayey soil and was so disgusted at what happened that she wrote an article about it for the *Rural New Yorker* called "A Nightmare of Mulch." There were three counts against the method, said she: One, the soil stayed wet. Two, it took her, I don't know how long but an improbable time, to spread the long awkward hay over just one small portion of the garden. Three, hay doesn't kill weeds.

I've already said something about wet hard soil and handling loose hay. Her third objection, about the weeds, came from the fact that the hay was full of vetch seeds and this is one of the few things which come through the mulch.

When she wrote this article there were already thousands of gardeners using my method and swearing by it. In a letter which I received from her she said that she had read an article of mine in the *Rural New Yorker* saying this; in other words, the method was obviously showing good results for many who were trying it and she knew it.

She might well just have written her own experience and stopped there, which would have warned others not to dump great quantities of hay full of vetch seeds on wet, cold, clayey soil. But she tried something which was new to her, made some mistakes, and then damned the whole thing publicly.

But her outburst did more good than harm; there was quite a lot of indignation among the elect. A periodical in Indiana had a two-page article, beginning: "When I read 'A Nightmare of Mulch' . . . I WAS SIMPLY HORRIFIED." He went on to say that the previous year his doctor had told him that he "would never push a garden plow again" on account of a heart ailment. Then he read an article of mine about year-round mulch, got my book and adopted the idea. The rest of the two pages were filled with his success and his delight, and great concern for fear the nightmare article would discourage others.

It may have halted some timid souls but indignant letters

poured in to the paper (including one from me, naturally) and many of them were published. The managing editor said, a year or so later, that nothing they had ever printed through his years with the paper had produced anything like so much interest and excitement as the nightmare outburst. The paper, I believe, sold a few hundred copies of my book as a by-product.

Now I am reminded of another assumption I made once, too early in the game. It was in my second or third year of gardening, during those sinful years when I was using chemical fertilizers and poisoning many of the things I grew. One day I stood looking at a large, handsome head of cabbage and said to myself: I've done some things in my life which I thought were worth while and were good, beneficial, *right,* but I guess in every case I could have found somebody who wouldn't have agreed. At last (I was looking fondly at the head of cabbage), at last I've done something about which there can be no argument; there may be bigger heads, but no one would say that I haven't produced something which has value, and is perfect in its small way.

But you see the snag, the wrong conclusion: the poor thing had been poisoned.

The sins of the experts in the flower world are legion, not that they are wrong and I am right, but because they state their opinions and theories as facts. I'm not going into detail here; it's bad enough to have my blood pressure go up when I think about vegetables. Flowers should bring us nothing but serene and pleasant thoughts.

I do feel sometimes that I would enjoy it if I could corner a few professors in a room from which they couldn't escape and ask them some questions. Such as: Before you wrote that one mustn't mulch the ground around bulbs until after the ground is frozen, how many years had you tried keeping them under a year-round mulch? Before you said it was next to impossible to grow gardenias successfully in an ordinary household, how many had you tried to grow? How many years did you mulch iris before you said that one

. . . . If I had my way I would make her write on the blackboard one hundred times: "Speech is silver, Silence is gold."

mustn't?

But there wouldn't be much satisfaction in this. I can savor vengeance to the last drop when I'm only thinking about it, but when my victim is there, in front of me, getting more and more embarrassed, to my annoyance I find myself feeling sorry for him.

There is, however, one woman lecturer who made such an ignorant, careless statement that I think she should be taught a lesson. I don't remember her name and if I did I wouldn't tell you; she doesn't deserve that much punishment. She said from a platform that tulip bulbs do not multiply. Although this surely misled very few, if I had my way I would make her write on the blackboard one hundred times: "Speech is silver; silence is gold."

Speaking of flowers, when we moved to Connecticut thirty years ago, my mother had a cottage built near our house and was in complete charge of the flower-beds, in both our yard and hers. She placed them here and there—near both houses, against the barn, with several on the lawn.

Some people who thought they were better informed than we were said that this was not only old fashioned but also made a lot of extra work, for the grass was always creeping into the beds and this meant frequent clipping, if the edges were to be kept neat looking.

Then, last summer, my sister came up with a splendid

solution which is so simple that it seems absurd that one of us hadn't thought of it long ago, and here it is: all around the edge of the long, rather narrow bed of tulips we placed, on top of the grass, a border of newspapers, magazines, card board, and other like material, then entirely covered all this with some half-rotted hay.

This paper can be made whatever width you think best; just be sure that it is wide enough for the lawn mower to cut along the border without getting too close to the flowers. Or you could, of course, cover the papers with dirt, and if the former are thick enough, it will be a few years, I should think, before they rot sufficiently for the grass to begin to get through. And if there are weed-seeds in the dirt, it doesn't matter; their roots are going to be thoroughly discouraged when they get down to a thick mat of paper. This trick is a great deal easier than burying strips of metal along the bor-der of flower beds to defeat the grass and, better still, it is in-finitely more effective. On top of all that, it doesn't cost a cent.

15

If you would be happy all your life

If you would be happy for a week take a wife; if you would be happy for a month kill a pig; but if you would be happy all your life, plant a garden.

That is a Chinese proverb and is true, of course, only for those who have the "soul" of a gardener. Others, perhaps, don't even see the miracle of a growing plant, let alone enjoy giving it a helping hand.

It is difficult to see how anyone can take just a little speck and put it in the ground and not be slightly startled when it begins to make a plant. The first year that I attempted a garden I went out one morning to look at the spot where I had put some early seeds and there was a row of tiny green, so straight and so purposeful that it couldn't be just weeds. I looked at the marker, then ran into the house to get my sister. She followed me out, expecting, from my excitement, goodness knows what. I showed her the little miracle, exclaiming:

"Look!"

"What are they?" she asked.

"Radishes!" I answered in, I suppose, a tone of awe.

Puzzled at my manner, she asked "But—what did you plant there?"

"Radishes," I said meekly, realizing now that I was overreacting to a well known phenomenon.

But I wasn't cured. After thirty years of growing things I still feel some stirring of surprise, gratitude and respect when seeds lie patiently in an envelope, doing nothing at all until you throw them in the dirt, then, never making a mistake, never once growing a carrot if the envelope says "lettuce," doing exactly what you expect of them.

Here's another miracle. Do you grow annual phlox? If you do you know all about the various colors and innumerable designs. How on earth does each little blossom decide to be just those particular colors with so many details and differing from all the others? It is mysterious enough that lilacs are certain shapes and colors and roses quite others, but all these variations in just one family of flowers are, to me, staggering.

There is also the feeling of accomplishment in the garden. You toss a few seeds on the ground and when they come bursting forth you say to yourself: Just see what I did! Who doesn't like that feeling?

What if they don't come up at all? Well, it wasn't your fault, was it? If you clean the house and it still looks dusty, if you burn the dinner, if you drive a nail and hit your finger, whom can you blame but yourself? But if a seed doesn't sprout maybe it was too old, maybe—you can think up quite a few reasons which take the blame from your shoulders.

But whether you accept the responsibility or not you are likely to investigate, try to find out what went wrong, and perhaps learn something. If you undertake to grow things you can scarcely avoid using your brain now and then, and this is a pleasure, once you try it. Many of our activities are automatic; we go along, day after day, behaving as we always have and/or as others are behaving, seldom asking "Why?" But if you have a garden you can hardly escape questions, can hardly get away from some attempt to find an answer now and then. This will keep your mind exercised, keep it from stagnating altogether.

Another desirable by-product of gardening is the physical exercise one gets, in the fresh air and sunshine. Did you ever try doing it barefooted? I like the feeling of grass or earth or mulch under my bare feet. Doctors tell us this is good for the nerves and whose nerves couldn't do with a little help nowadays?

If you have the soul of a gardener, not for anything would you work with gloves on. The feel of the warm earth, not too dry, not too wet, is something no one can ever describe to you if you don't get it, yourself. The smell of it and the unassuming wonder of what it accomplishes fill you with a kind of faith. You may not actually think about it, but if you do, it probably comes out something like this: if anything so simple, so humble, can do so much, there is hope for man, no matter how determined he is to destroy himself.

I like to sit on a bale of hay and listen to the songs of gratitude all around me. So many things are thanking me for making their duties less strenuous. The earthworms are grateful to me for giving them a pleasant moist spot under the hay in which to do their work; no more baked soil or worry about drought. I feel like the boss of a factory who has torn down the old ramshackle building and has put up a comfortable one, full of sunshine.

All the plants thank me for keeping out their enemies, the weeds, and that makes me feel like the head of a nation who has peacefully done away with the enemy simply by not having any, rather than making everyone struggle and

. . . *"I did my share. Let me pass, please."*

fight to hold his own, trying to crowd each other out and to grab some part of the nourishment for himself.

But when they all join in a chorus of thanks to me for not poisoning them I am embarrassed and even a little annoyed. For now I feel like a mother whose child is thanking her for not spanking him when there has been no reason whatever for punishing him, and I say crossly:

"Why would I poison you, for goodness' sake?"

As I sit on the hay I marvel a little. It seems only yesterday that the ground was frozen and now it looks like a young, eager forest. Ambitious, but so calm and quiet! Full of great plans, but not in a hurry. Each anxious to do its best, but not trying to outdo the others.

Can all this be true or do I imagine it? Is achievement possible, then, without envy, frustration, rush? I go to walk around the flower beds, one after another. A beauty contest? No, just beauty.

Here, too, are the busy earthworms, behaving as if they didn't know that the rest of the world was running hog wild. And probably they wouldn't care, in any case. When they die and go to their Heaven and Saint Peter asks them what they did on earth to deserve admission they will answer with quiet dignity:

"I did my share. Let me pass, please."

Index

Index

Index

One hard lesson we gardeners have to learn is to be hard-hearted; thinning is a painful process. (See page 117)